Introducing Meteor

Josh Robinson
Aaron Gray
David Titarenco

Apress®

Introducing Meteor

ISBN-13 (pbk): 978-1-4302-6836-9

ISBN-13 (electronic): 978-1-4302-6835-2

Managing Director: Welmoed Spahr
Lead Editor: Ben Renow-Clarke
Technical Reviewer: Adam Gamble
Editorial Board: Steve Anglin, Pramila Balen, Louise Corrigan, Jim DeWolf, Jonathan Gennick, Robert Hutchinson, Celestin Suresh John, Michelle Lowman, James Markham, Susan McDermott, Matthew Moodie, Jeffrey Pepper, Douglas Pundick, Ben Renow-Clarke, Gwenan Spearing
Coordinating Editor: Melissa Maldonado
Compositor: SPi Global
Indexer: SPi Global
Artist: SPi Global

Distributed to the book trade worldwide by Springer Science+Business Media New York, 233 Spring Street, 6th Floor, New York, NY 10013. Phone 1-800-SPRINGER, fax (201) 348-4505, e-mail orders-ny@springer-sbm.com, or visit www.springer.com. Apress Media, LLC is a California LLC and the sole member (owner) is Springer Science + Business Media Finance Inc (SSBM Finance Inc). SSBM Finance Inc is a **Delaware** corporation.

For information on translations, please e-mail rights@apress.com, or visit www.apress.com.

Apress and friends of ED books may be purchased in bulk for academic, corporate, or promotional use. eBook versions and licenses are also available for most titles. For more information, reference our Special Bulk Sales–eBook Licensing web page at www.apress.com/bulk-sales.

Any source code or other supplementary materials referenced by the author in this text is available to readers at www.apress.com. For detailed information about how to locate your book's source code, go to www.apress.com/source-code/.

Contents at a Glance

Contents

About the Authors

Josh Robinson is a code craftsman and freelance developer who thrives on cutting edge technology. His love for coding began with the blue glow of a second hand Commodore 64 and has continued into his career developing for the modern web. He can be stalked at JoshRobinson.com or on Twitter @JoshRobinson.

Aaron Gray is a software engineer who has run a freelance consultancy, built an acquired startup, and as the lead instructor, transitioned a 6 month programming bootcamp curriculum from Ruby to JavaScript. He contributes to OSS – namely Susy and other side projects – organizes several meetups, and speaks where they'll let him. In his spare time, Aaron can likely be found reading science fiction, quoting Jos Whedon, or taking a nap. You can reach him on Twitter at @aaronagray.

David Titarenco is a software engineer from sunny Los Angeles. He is a proponent of open source and has contributed to a number of high-profile projects like Google Go and the Java Kilim microthreading library. A self-proclaimed startup addict, he's founded several ventures in the past decade and you can keep up with him at http://dvt.name or on Twitter: @davvv.

He graduated with a magna cum laude Bachelor of Arts from UCLA, where he studied Philosophy and Mathematical Logic. Go Bruins!

About the Technical Reviewer

Adam Gamble is a professional web developer currently working for Isotope 11 in Birmingham, AL. He has over 10 years' experience building web applications for everything from startups to multiple Fortune 500 companies. His passion for technology has enabled him to turn a hobby into a career that he loves.

Introduction

Introducing Meteor walks you through building top-quality web apps in a fraction of the time using an application platform built for the modern web. Meteor is a web development platform that aims at giving developers the tools they need to build better apps faster.

One of my favorite things about Meteor is how easy it is for someone who is completely new to web development to get started making amazing, and impressive, web apps. That is why this book starts with a crash course in web development. The first chapter covers all the basic elements of a web app and gives you a foundation for getting started with Meteor or any other web development framework. If you are already familiar with web development you can easily jump right into Meteor and skip the crash course.

After the basics are covered it is time to get a development environment all setup. Not only will this let you follow along with the examples in the book, but you will be able to play with the code as well. The best way to learn is to try things out and see what works and what doesn't.

Building an app really comes down to modeling data, building interfaces to display and interact with the data, and connecting the two together. The next three chapters cover how to build interfaces using spacebar templates, making your interface react to and change data, and dealing with the data in a backend database. All things Meteor makes very easy.

An app is no good if you can't show it off so we wrap things up by helping you secure your app and release it on the world. Meteor is a full stack application platform that makes it easy to build powerful, realtime web apps quickly. Web apps have come a long way since the 1990's, but they still require a lot of time, specialized knowledge and complex setups. Meteor changes that.

CHAPTER 1

Web Development Crash Course

Meteor is a platform for web development; as such it relies on the standard building blocks of the web. Before jumping into building an app with Meteor, it is important to cover what technologies we will be using. Readers familiar with web development may be able to skip this chapter, but for someone just getting started this chapter will lay the needed groundwork

HTML – The Structure

HTML (HyperText Markup Language) is at the center of web development and is the starting point of every web page. HTML was created in the early '90s as a way to describe and share interlinking documents across the Internet. Although web technology and how we use it has evolved over the years HTML remains a cornerstone.

When we visit a page on the Internet our browser is sending a request to the server for an HTML document. These documents are simple text files and can be edited with any plain text editor. But they contain instructions that describe the structure of the content to a browser. This lets a browser display the content in a nice format and load any additional resources, such as images, that it may need.

Tags and Attributes

Elements are the basic unit in HTML and they are described using tags. An HTML element is a block of content that is wrapped with an opening tag and a matching closing tag that give meaning to the content. An example is the h1 tag that tells the browser that the content inside is a top-level header.

```
<h1>Hello World</h1>
```

You can recognize tags by the angle brackets <> that surround the tag name. Most tags have an opening and a closing tag. You can tell a tag is a closing tab because it will include a slash (/) inside of the angle brackets <> before the tag name. Here are a couple examples of opening tags and their closing tags:

```
<h1></h1>
<h2></h2>
<p></p>
<div></div>
```

One of the things that make HTML extremely flexible is the ability to nest elements. This means that each element can contain other elements in a tree-like structure. For example an ordered list can contain many items inside it.

```
<ol>
  <li>Item 1</li>
  <li>Item 2</li>
</ol>
```

By parsing this markup the browser can understand the content. The markup describes a list with two items in it, so the browser by default will show "Item 1" and "Item 2" on two lines with the number 1 next to the first item and the number 2 next to the second item. Later, we will learn how to change the default styles with CSS. Just using HTML, however, your browser can present the content in a meaningful way.

Tags give the browser a basic idea of what the content is, but you usually want to give it a little more information. This is done using attributes. Attributes are added to the opening tag and each tag can contain multiple attributes. Some tags even require specific attributes to work. A couple attributes can be used on any tag though. The most common are id and class. Let's take a look at an example.

```
<ul id="messages" class="activity">
  <li class="message">Hello</li>
  <li class="message">World</li>
</ul>
```

As you can see in the example, attributes come after the tag name and are in the format name="value". Multiple attributes are separated by a space.

The id attribute is used to give a name to a specific element. This means that in our example above, the list is named "messages". Because an id identifies a specific element it should be unique and only used once in a document. Modern browsers do a really good job of dealing with invalid HTML, however, and the page will still load if you use an id in multiple places.

Classes are different from ids in that they can be used on multiple elements. In addition an element can also have multiple classes. Ids and elements have a one-to-one relationship while classes and elements have a many-to-many relationship. In order to add multiple classes to an element you pass a space-separated list as the value of the class attribute.

```
<ul id="messages" class="activity">
  <li class="message">Hello</li>
  <li class="messages active">World</li>
</ul>
```

Now that we know the basic building blocks of an HTML document it is time to see how they are structured.

Document Basics

Every HTML document starts out with the same basic structure. Here is an example of the classic hello world example in HTML:

```
<!DOCTYPE HTML>
<html>
  <head>
    <title>Hello World</title>
  </head>
  <body>
    <p>Hello World</p>
  </body>
</html>
```

Every HTML document starts with a DOCTYPE tag.

```
<!DOCTYPE HTML>
```

The doctype tells your browser what version of HTML it should expect. Over the years this has varied but with HTML5, the latest HTML standard, the doctype is simply HTML.

After the doctype, the entire document is wrapped in an html tag.

```
<!DOCTYPE HTML>
<html>
  ...
</html>
```

This gives your browser a root to start building its tree of elements from.

3

Inside the html tag you have two sections, head and body.

```
<!DOCTYPE HTML>
<html>
  <head>
    ...
  </head>
  <body>
    ...
  </body>
</html>
```

The head tag contains any information about the document that your browser needs to know but isn't part of the page's content. This usually includes meta tags used for SEO (Search Engine Optimization), link tags used to tell your browser where to find external style sheets, and script tags to either load an external JavaScript file or include some inline JavaScript. In our example we are only using the title tag, which is used to set the title on your browser's window or tab.

```
<head>
  <title>Hello World</title>
</head>
```

Below the head section we have the body. This is where we put the content for our page. In our simple example this only contains a single p (paragraph) tag wrapping the text "Hello World".

```
<body>
  <p>Hello World</p>
</body>
```

Web frameworks such as Meteor always produce this same structure but usually simplify the process so you don't have to create each page manually.

Common Tags

The browser has a set of standard tags that it understands. Here is a list of some of the most common HTML5 tags and when they should be used.

Link Tag (link)

Link tags tell the browser about an external resource, most commonly a stylesheet.

```
<link href="//netdna.bootstrapcdn.com/bootstrap/3.1.0/css/bootstrap.min.css"
rel="stylesheet">
```

Style Tag (style)

The style tag is used to include inline CSS. In most cases you will put your styles in a separate file and include them in your HTML document using the link tag, but you will often see a style tag in examples and very simple documents.

```
<style type="text/css">
  body {
    background-color: lemonchiffon;
  }
</style>
```

Script Tag (script)

The script tag can be used to either include a JavaScript file from an external source or write inline JavaScript.

```
<script src="//netdna.bootstrapcdn.com/bootstrap/3.1.0/js/bootstrap.min.js">
</script>
```

Or

```
<script>
  alert("Hello World");
</script>
```

Heading Tags (h1, h2, h3, h4, h5, h6)

Heading tags are used to show up to six levels of document headings. The most important is h1 and the least is h6. Default browser styles will show the content of each heading in different sizes with h1 being the largest and h6 the smallest. It is important to note that the heading tags and their levels play a role in SEO.

```
<h1>Most important</h1>
<h3>Less important</h3>
<h6>Least important</h6>
```

Paragraph Tag (p)

This tag wraps a paragraph of text as its name suggests.

```
<p>
  Donec a massa a quam pellentesque sollicitudin. Donec condimentum egestas
  nisl ac imperdiet.
</p>
<p>
  Lorem ipsum dolor sit amet, consectetur adipiscing elit.
</p>
```

Anchor Tag (a)

An anchor tag defines a hyperlink to another resource. This tag is what makes the Internet. In order to point the link at another document you have to set the href (HyperText Reference) attribute.

```
<a href="http://www.meteor.com">Meteor</a>
```

Generic Tags (div, span)

These tags are what you use when you don't have a better option, which means they are used a lot. div is a general container and span is for general text. They are very similar but act differently, as we will see in the section on the box model.

```
<div>
  <span>Hello World</span>
</div>
```

Image Tag (img)

The Internet would be pretty boring without the img tag. This is the tag that tells the browser where images should be inserted into the document and where they can be found. For the img tag to work it needs to have the src (source) attribute set to the location of the image.

```
<img src="/logo.png" />
```

The image tag does not surround other content so it does not have a closing tag. Instead it has the slash at the end of the opening tag. Tags like the img tag are called self-closing tags.

Section Tags (section, nav, article, aside, header, footer, address, main)

With HTML5, several section tags were added so developers wouldn't have to use the div tag for everything. All the section tags act the same as the div tag but give the markup more meaning.

```
<body>
  <header>
    <img src="/logo.png" />
    <nav>
      <a href="/">Home</a>
      <a href="/about">About Us</a>
    </nav>
  </header>
```

```
<main>
  <section id="articles">
    <article>
      <p>Lorem ipsum dolor sit amet, consectetur adipiscing elit.</p>
      <aside>
        <p>Related content</p>
      </aside>
    </article>
  </section>
</main>
<footer>
  <p>Some Links</p>
  <address>
    123 Main St.
    Somewhere, Good
  </address>
</footer>
</body>
```

List Tags (ol, ul, li)

Lists are incredibly common. We make lists of everything. For example this is a list of common HTML tags. The ol (ordered list) and ul (unordered list) tags let us tell the browser what type of list we are trying to make. Inside of each list tag we wrap each item in a li (list item) tag. The ol tag will put each list item on its own line with a number to the left starting at 1. The ul tag will also list each item on its own line but instead of a number, it will put a bullet next to the items. Because these default styles do not fit in with most of the uses of the list tags they are usually changed using CSS.

```
<ol id="leaderboard">
  <li>First Place</li>
  <li>Second Place</li>
  <li>Third Place</li>
</ol>

<ul id="fruits">
  <li>Oranges</li>
  <li>Apples</li>
</ul>
```

Table Tags (table, thead, tbody, tfoot, tr, td, th)

The table tags are used to display tabular data. Before the creation of CSS tables were used for layout. Do not do that. Now that we have CSS, the table tags should only be used for tables of data. The entire table is enclosed in a table tag with thead, tbody, and tfoot defining the different sections of the table. Inside any section you will have a tr (table row) tag containing a number of either th (table header cell) tags or td (table data cell) tags.

```
<table id="children">
  <thead>
    <tr>
      <th>First Name</th>
      <th>Last Name</th>
      <th>Age</th>
    </tr>
  </thead>
  <tbody>
    <tr>
      <td>Andraya</td>
      <td>Robinson</td>
      <td>5 years</td>
    </tr>
    <tr>
      <td>Leana</td>
      <td>Robinson</td>
      <td>2 Months</td>
    </tr>
  </tbody>
</table>
```

Form Tags (form, fieldset, legend, label, input, button, select, option, textarea)

Any time we want to get information from a user we will need to use a form. Forms are wrapped in a form tag and contain labels, inputs, buttons, select boxes, and textareas.

```
<form action="/new/session" method="post">
  <fieldset>
    <legend>Login</legend>

    <label for="login-email">Email Address</label>
    <input id="login-email" type="email" name="email" />

    <label for="login-user-name">User Name</label>
    <input id="login-user-name" type="text" name="user-name" />

    <label for="login-password">Password</label>
    <input id="login-password" type="password" name="password" />
  </fieldset>

  <input type="submit" value="Login"/>
</form>
```

Linking to Other Resources

A web page is built around an HTML document but would be boring if it didn't include other resources and link to other documents. It is the combination of HTML documents, stylesheets, JavaScript files, images, and links to other pages that make the web such a dynamic, interesting, and powerful technology.

The URL

Different resources are loaded into a page using different HTML tags but they all point to resources using a URL (Uniform Resource Locator). A URL is made up of several parts that describe where a resource can be found.

The parts of a URL are the scheme, host, port, path, query_string and fragment. They are combined into a single string using the following format:

```
scheme://host:port/path?query_string#fragment
```

Scheme (http, https)

The scheme tells the browser what protocol to use. For web pages this is usually either http (HyperText Transfer Protocol) or https (HyperText Transfer Protocol Secure). When you see a lock in your browser this is because the protocol is https, and the connection to the server is encrypted. Browsers will default to http for the protocol and only use https when told to do so since not all sites support https.

Host (`www.example.com`)

The host is usually a domain name, which is a human friendly way to refer to a specific server or set of servers on the Internet. When you type `www.google.com` in your browser it is telling it to retrieve an HTML document from Google's servers. If you know the IP address of a server you can use that as the host instead of a domain name. A useful trick when developing is to use `localhost` as the host, which will tell your browser to look for the resources on the computer it is running on.

Port (80, 443, 3000)

Each server can serve documents from different port numbers. The port is usually determined by the protocol used, with http using port 80 and https using port 443. Because of this people normally do not specify port numbers in URLs. The most common case for using alternate ports is when developing a website. For example when you start a Meteor server it does not listen on port 80 by default, instead it listens on port 3000. So to view a Meteor app at port 3000 on your local computer you would use the URL `http://localhost:3000`.

Path (/users)

The path tells the browser what file to request from the host. The format is very similar to the filesystem on your local computer. If the path is left out of the URL or it ends in a forward slash (/) the server will normally look for an index.html file to respond with. Many web servers are case sensitive and will require the path to match the capitalization of the file you are referencing. When the server responding to the request is a web framework, most HTML documents are dynamically generated. This allows the server to look at the path and build the HTML document on demand. We will see how powerful this can be when we take a look at routing in Meteor.

Query String (?term=Meteor&page=1)

The query string is a way of giving the server extra information that it can use to generate the HTML document. For example we may be requesting a search page so our path is /search. But we want to search for a specific term so we pass a query string of ?term=Meteor. When we want to go to the second page of results we can tell the server by using a query string of ?term=Meteor&page=2. How the query string is used is up to the server and most of the time you can add unused items to the query string and they will be ignored.

Fragment (#id)

Fragments are not sent to the server and were originally used to jump to an HTML element with a specific id. As web apps began to do more on the client side, the fragment has been used to pass information to the browser without sending additional requests to the server.

Relative URLs

What do you do if you don't know the entire URL? For example what if you are building an app on your local computer and using localhost but when it goes live you are going to host it on a server in the cloud somewhere? To handle cases like this HTML lets you use relative URLs that use the current document as a base for where to find the resource. When creating a web app you almost always want to use relative URLs.

Current Host

If you want the URL to refer to the server your current HTML document was served from you can simply leave off the scheme, host, and protocol. For example if I want to link to the about page from the home page I can use:

```
<a href="/about">About Us</a>
```

Using the forward slash tells the browser to request the document from the same host as the current document but ignore the path of the current document. Leaving off the forward slash will base the request off the current host and path. For example if I am on the /company page I use the following to refer to the /company/about page:

```
<a href="about">About Us</a>
```

Current Page

Sometimes you want a link to point to a different part of the same page. This is what the fragment is used for. Creating a link to a fragment only is unique because it does not reload the page. Instead it changes the address bar and jumps to the element with an id matching the fragment. With HTML5 you can achieve something similar with the History API. Before HTML5 web apps used the fragment routing (also called hash routing) to change the content without refreshing the page. A link to an about section on the current page would look like this:

```
<a href="#about">About Us</a>
```

CSS – The Style

Structuring your content is cool and all but without CSS (Cascading Style Sheets) it will be ugly, very ugly. CSS provides a way to cleanly separate the look and formatting of a site from its structure. Changing a stylesheet for a web page can completely change its look and feel. To get an idea of how completely, take a look at http://www.csszengarden.com. The CSS Zen Garden lets you view the same markup with different CSS applied.

Getting It into Your Document

CSS can be kept in a separate file and loaded into your document using the link tag or can be included inline using the style tag. For most sites it makes sense to keep the stylesheets separate so they can be included on multiple pages on your site. Let's take a look at how you can include a separate stylesheet on the same host as your HTML document.

```
<html>
  <head>
    <link href="/styles.css" rel="stylesheet">
  </head>
  <body>
    ...
  </body>
</html>
```

If you do need to include some page-specific styles you can add them directly to the head section of your HTML document.

```
<html>
  <head>
    <style type="text/css">
      body {
        background-color: lemonchiffon;
      }
    </style>
  </head>
  <body>
    ...
  </body>
</html>
```

Selectors

CSS styles a web page by applying properties to HTML elements that match a selector.

```
selector {
  property: value;
}
```

The selector is a combination of tag names, ids, and classes that can be used to target specific elements on a page.

Tags

A tag selector simply uses the tag name without any additional markup to select any element on the page of that type. For example this is the CSS to make every h1 tag on the page red:

```
<html>
  <head>
    <style type="text/css">
      h1 {
        color: red;
      }
    </style>
  <head>
  <body>
    <h1>This is red</h1>
    <h2>This is not red</h2>
    <h1>This is red</h1>
  <body>
</html>
```

Ids

You can target an element with a specific id by using the hash symbol followed by the id. This follows the same convention as URL fragments. When using an id on its own to target it will only match one element since an id can only belong to a single element. Here is how you would set the background color of a nav tag with an id of menu to black and its text to white:

```
<html>
  <head>
    <style type="text/css">
      #menu {
        background-color: black;
        color: white;
      }
    </style>
  <head>
  <body>
    <nav id="menu">
      <a href="/">Home</a>
    </nav>
  <body>
</html>
```

Classes

A class is denoted by a period preceding the class name. Since a class can be applied to many elements, every element with a matching class will have the properties applied to it. This is how you would set the background color to yellow for every item with the highlight class:

```
<html>
  <head>
    <style type="text/css">
      .highlight {
        background-color: yellow;
      }
    </style>
  <head>
  <body>
    <h1 class="highlight header">This is highlighted</h1>
    <h1 class="header">This is not highlighted</h1>
    <h1 class="highlight">This is highlighted</h1>
  <body>
</html>
```

Pseudo Classes

Pseudo classes are different than other types of selectors because they are dependent on the state of an element. A good example of this is the :hover pseudo class. It is applied any time the mouse hovers over the element. Pseudo classes are usually used in combination with other selectors. We will see how to combine selectors in the next section. For now, let's take a look at how we would set the background to red on any list item that has the mouse over it.

```html
<html>
  <head>
    <style type="text/css">
      li:hover {
        background-color: red;
      }
    </style>
  <head>
  <body>
    <ul>
      <li>Item 1</li>
      <li>Item 2</li>
      <li>Item 3</li>
    </ul>
  <body>
</html>
```

Compound Selectors

To add some precision to our selectors we can combine them. In order to target an element that is both an h1 and has a highlight class we put the tag selector and class selector together as one selector with no space.

```
h1.highlight {}
```

We can target a multiple selectors by using a comma-separated list.

```
h1, h2, h3 {}
```

This also works when combining selectors.

```
h1.highlight,
a.highlight {}
```

We can even target elements based on what elements they are nested in. This example will select any a tags with an active class that are nested anywhere under the #menu element:

```
#menu a.active {}
```

If we want to restrict the selection to a direct child of an element we can use >, which will limit the scope.

```
#menu > a
```

Order Matters

By now you may be wondering what happens when multiple selectors with conflicting properties target the same element. This is where the cascading part of CSS comes in. The style rules are applied in the order they appear in the style sheet. As new styles are applied they will overwrite previous styles. This lets us put generic rules early on and overwrite them with more specific rules later. Here, we are setting all h1 elements to be red and then setting any h1 elements with an active class to be green.

```
<html>
  <head>
    <style type="text/css">
      h1 {
        color: red;
      }
      h1.active {
        color: green;
      }
    </style>
  <head>
  <body>
    <h1>This is red</h1>
    <h1 class="active">This is green</h1>
    <h1>This is red</h1>
  <body>
</html>
```

The only exception you need to watch out for is !important. This keyword can be added to an attribute causing it to be applied even if another style attempts to overwrite it later. In order for another style to over write one with !important set it must also set !important. Since !important causes attributes to be applied in an unexpected order it should be used sparingly.

Staying Semantic

When styling your web pages, you will often need to add additional ids and classes to your HTML markup. It is important to remember that those ids and classes should describe what the content is and not how it should look. Style requirements can change but what an element is should stay consistent. If we were to add a .blue class to an element and then style it blue with CSS it would work. But if we decide that element should be red and we change it in the CSS it won't match up with the name of the class. However if we name the element what it is and target that with CSS, the color can change all the time and everything will still match up.

CSS Frameworks

When working with CSS you will find yourself doing the same things over and over. CSS Frameworks help by providing a bunch of pre-written styles that we can apply to our HTML document by following the naming conventions they use. Bootstrap (http://getbootstrap.com) is the most common but several others are gaining in popularity including Semantic (http://semantic-ui.com), Foundation (http://foundation.zurb.com), and Pure (http://purecss.io). In addition to making your CSS easier to manage they can also make your app look decent without much additional design work.

JavaScript – The Behavior

JavaScript is what brings our web apps to life. It can tie into and manipulate both the site's structure and its style. It lets us listen for user actions and make our app respond to them. JavaScript takes a web page and turns it into an app. Modern browsers have a built-in logging function that we will be using to print to the browser's console. The console is a magical place where you can enter JavaScript code and the browser will execute it against the current page immediately. In most browsers you can access the console by right-clicking on a page and selecting "Inspect Element" to open the developer tools, and clicking on the console tab.

Where to Put Your Code

The script tag can be used to load external JavaScript files or write inline JavaScript. The script tags can go inside the head element or the body element. Many people like to keep their scripts in the head of a document so they can keep all external stylesheets and JavaScript files together. However, the best place to put your script tags is at the bottom of your HTML document, right before the closing body tag. This lets your browser load the bulk of the HTML document before processing the scripts. The performance gain is small, but if you have a lot of JavaScript to load and are on a slow connection it can make a difference.

```
<html>
  <head>
    <title>Hello World</title>
  </head>
  <body>
    <h1>Hello World</h1>
    <script src="/app.js"></script>
  </body>
</html>
```

Inline JavaScript is written between the open script tag and the closing script tag. This is often used to initialize external libraries that have already been loaded.

```
<html>
  <head>
    <title>Hello World</title>
  </head>
  <body>
    <h1>Hello World</h1>
    <script>
      alert("hello world");
    </script>
  </body>
</html>
```

Dealing with Data

Moving data around is what programming is all about. In order to help the computer understand what kind of data we are working with, we use several basic datatypes. These basic building blocks can be combined to create more complex data structures.

Primitive Types

These are simple base types that are common in most programming languages. They are used to describe the most basic units of logic: text, numbers, and truth.

String

A string is a collection of letters and is denoted by single or double quotes.

```
<script>
  console.log("This is a string");
</script>
```

Numeric

A numeric type can be an Integer such as 1 or a Double like 1.1, but they both act the same.

```
<script>
  console.log(42);
</script>
```

Boolean

Boolean values are ones that only have two possible values, true or false, and are denoted with those key words.

```
<script>
  console.log(true);
  console.log(false);
</script>
```

Complex Types

Complex types can contain other primitive and complex types. They are the glue used to combine data into useful structures. By using complex types to combine primitive types we can create advanced data structures to handle any case.

Arrays

An array is simply a list of other pieces of data. Arrays are enclosed in square brackets [ ] and contain a comma-separated list of other datatypes. The datatypes in the array can be any valid type and can be mixed and matched.

```
<script>
  console.log([1,2, 'a', 'b', true]);
</script>
```

Since they can include any valid datatype they can also include other arrays.

```
<script>
  console.log([[1,2,3],['a','b','c'], true]);
</script>
```

Objects

Objects in JavaScript are simple key–value structures built using curly braces.

```
<script>
  console.log({
    "a": 1,
    "b": 2
  });
</script>
```

You can then get the data back out using dot notation or passing the key to the object in square brackets.

```
<script>
  var alphabet = {
    "a": 1,
    "b": 2,
    "c": 3,
    "d": 4
  };
  console.log(alphabet.a); // this will output 1
  console.log(alphabet["b"]); // this will output 2
</script>
```

Variables

Variables store data and give it a name that can be used later. You can think of it as a bunch of boxes with labels on them storing you data. Variables are usually defined with the var keyword to keep them confined to the section of code where they are defined. Setting a variable without the var keyword puts it in the global namespace, which can cause conflicts if you are not careful. The value of a variable is set using a single equal sign with the value on the right.

```
<script>
  var x = 3;
  var y = 4;
  console.log(x); // this will output 3
  console.log(y); // this will output 4
</script>
```

JSON

JavaScript Object Notation or JSON is an open standard for exchanging data as human readable text. It provides a simple way to store and transmit data in a format that both computers and humans can understand. To do this, our JavaScript data is converted into a string that conforms to a strict version of the data notation we used earlier.

Modern browsers provide a way to easily convert JSON to JavaScript data and back again using the JSON global object. Let's look at a few examples.

```
<script>
  var userData = {
    "firstName": "Josh",
    "lastName": "Robinson",
    "active": true
  };
```

```
    var json = JSON.stringify(userData);
    console.log(json); // This will output the JSON string

    var data = JSON.parse(json);
    console.log(data); // This will output the original userData object
</script>
```

Math and Operators

Like most programming languages JavaScript is really good at math. It can do the usual addition, subtraction, multiplication, and division along with equality tests.

Math Operators

Addition and subtraction use the expected plus and minus signs while multiplication and division use the asterisk (*) and forward slash (/). As is most math notation parentheses can be used to control the order of operation.

```
<script>
  var apples = 42;
  var oranges = 7;

  // addition
  console.log(apples + oranges); // This will output 49

  // subtraction
  console.log(apples - oranges); // This will output 35

  // multiplication
  console.log(apples * oranges); // This will output 294

  // division
  console.log(apples / oranges); // This will output 6
</script>
```

Comparison Operators

A comparison operator will compare two values and return a Boolean (true/false) value. Comparison is not limited to Numeric datatypes; in fact, most datatypes can be compared. Let's look at some examples.

```
<script>
  // equal (==)
  console.log( 1 == 2);      // This will output false
  console.log( 1 == "1");    // This will output true
  console.log( (4 - 3) == 1); // This will output true
```

```
// strict equal (===)
console.log( 1 === 2);      // This will output false
console.log( 1 === "1");    // This will output false
console.log( (4 - 3) === 1); // This will output true

// not equal (!=)
console.log( 1 != 2);       // This will output true
console.log( 1 != 1);       // This will output false
console.log( (4 - 3) != 1); // This will output false

// strict not equal (!==)
console.log( 1 !== 2);       // This will output true
console.log( 1 !== "1");     // This will output true
console.log( (4 - 3) !== 1); // This will output false

// greater than (>)
console.log( 1 > 2);        // This will output false
console.log( 1 > 1);        // This will output false
console.log( (4 - 2) > 1);  // This will output true

// greater than or equal (>=)
console.log( 1 >= 2);       // This will output false
console.log( 1 >= 1);       // This will output true
console.log( (4 - 2) >= 1); // This will output true

// less than (<)
console.log( 1 < 2);        // This will output true
console.log( 1 < 1);        // This will output false
console.log( (4 - 2) < 1);  // This will output false

// less than or equal (<=)
console.log( 1 <= 2);       // This will output true
console.log( 1 <= 1);       // This will output true
console.log( (4 - 2) <= 1); // This will output false
</script>
```

Conditions

To control the flow of our program we need to have a way to execute code conditionally. The most common way to do this in JavaScript is with the if and if-else statements. The if statement starts with the if keyword and is followed by a condition in parentheses. If the condition evaluates to true then the code following the condition and enclosed in curly braces will be executed.

```
<script>
  var favoriteFood = "pizza";
  var age = 5;

  if ( age < 12 ) {
    favoriteFood = "icecream";
  }

  console.log("you are eating: ", favoriteFood); // This will output
  "you are eating: icecream"
</script>
```

Setting the favoriteFood variable at the beginning of the script and then changing it based on the condition is a bit cumbersome. What we really want to do is keep the decision logic in a single place. For this we can use if-else.

```
<script>
  var favoriteFood;
  var age = 5;

  if ( age < 12 ) {
    favoriteFood = "icecream";
  } else {
    favoriteFood = "pizza";
  }

  console.log("you are eating: ", favoriteFood); // This will output
  "you are eating: icecream"
</script>
```

If we need to add in more conditions we can do so using else-if statements.

```
<script>
  var favoriteFood;
  var age = 5;

  if (age <= 5) {
    favoriteFood = "chocolate";
  } else if ( age < 12 ) {
    favoriteFood = "icecream";
  } else {
    favoriteFood = "pizza";
  }

  console.log("you are eating: ", favoriteFood); // This will output
  "you are eating: chocolate"
</script>
```

As you can see, only the first matching condition is run when using else-if. Although you can add as many else-if statements into the condition the first statement must be an if by itself. The else acts as a catchall and is run if no other conditions match. It is optional but must come last if it is included.

Loops

In an app, there are many times when a loop can come in handy. For example if we needed to print the numbers 1 to 100 out to the console, then we could do it by hand and write 100 lines of code. Not only would this be a pain, it would also be hard to change. If the requirement changes to print 1 to 200 then we would have to write another 100 lines of code.

If we want to output the contents of an array to the page we will need a way to loop through the array and run some code on each value. In JavaScript we have two main types of loops, while loops and for loops.

While Loops

A while loop combines a conditional with a block of code, and will continually run the code as long as the condition is true.

```
<script>
  var i = 1;

  while (i <= 42) {
    console.log(i);
    i = i + 1;
  }
</script>
```

For Loops

A for loop acts as a counter and is passed a starting value, condition, and incrementer function.

```
<script>
  for (var i = 1; i <= 42; i++) {
    console.log(i);
  }
</script>
```

Using the length property of an array as the condition makes a for loop a great way to iterate over an array.

```
<script>
  var fruits = ["apples", "oranges", "bananas"];

  // We start i at 0 because arrays are 0 indexed, meaning the first item is
  in position 0
  for (var i = 0; i < fruits.length; i++) {
    console.log(fruits[i]);
  }
</script>
```

Functions

Functions are reusable blocks of code. In JavaScript, functions act the same as other pieces of data and can be stored in variables and passed as arguments to other functions. Functions can be defined with a name or as an anonymous function. Although there is some debate on which style is best, I prefer declaring functions anonymously and assigning them to variables. This lets me easily treat a function the same as any piece of data. Let's take a look at both ways of declaring a function.

```
<script>
  function square(x) {
    return x * x;
  }

  console.log(square(10)); // This will output 100

  var sqr = function (x) {
    return x * x;
  }

  console.log(sqr(30)); // This will output 900
</script>
```

There are two things we are doing in the previous example that we haven't covered yet. First of all we are invoking the function using parentheses and passing in arguments. Secondly we are telling the function to return a result. These two things combined let us deal with either the function itself or the result of the function.

```
<script>
  var sqr = function (x) {
    return x * x;
  }
```

```
console.log(sqr); // This will output the function sqr
console.log(sqr(30); // This will output the results of running the code
with a value of 30 for x
</script>
```

CoffeeScript

You may have noticed that the syntax for JavaScript has a lot of curly braces and semi-colons. Although JavaScript is the only language most browsers understand natively, we still have some options for a cleaner language. CoffeeScript (http://coffeescript.org) was designed to take the best parts of JavaScript, Ruby, Python, and functional programing languages and combine them into one nice clean language. In order to be compatible with browsers, CoffeeScript compiles into standard JavaScript. This means that after compiling CoffeeScript you can run it anywhere that you can run JavaScript and use any existing JavaScript libraries.

So why aren't we using CoffeeScript in this book? Although I love CoffeeScript, some people prefer to use plain JavaScript and I didn't want learning CoffeeScript to be a barrier to entry. Meteor does have great CoffeeScript support, though, and we will show how to get up and running with CoffeeScript on Meteor in our install section.

Summary

In this chapter we got a brief overview of the three main technologies that make the web possible. We learned how to structure our content with HTML, Style it with CSS, and make it come alive with JavaScript. Although we didn't dive deep into any one area, after reading this section you should have the groundwork in place to get started making amazing real-time apps with Meteor.

CHAPTER 2

Getting Started with Meteor

One of the strengths of Meteor is how quickly you can get started. With a little guidance, a beginner can have a Meteor development environment setup and their first app created in a matter of minutes. This chapter provides that guidance. It also covers some of the guiding principles of Meteor and what makes it different from other options.

The Seven Principles of Meteor

The Internet has made major advancements over the last couple decades. Yet most sites are built using aging techniques. Meteor focuses on creating modern apps for today not 20 years ago. To make sure its focus holds true, Meteor has developed seven guiding principles. These principles are really a definition of what a modern web framework should look like.

Data on the Wire

> *Don't send HTML over the network. Send data and let the client decide how to render it.*

> —docs.meteor.com

Early on, browsers could only render HTML. Initially, the HTML for a page was generated all at once, fully formed, on the server. As browsers advanced, they gained the ability to send requests back to the server and update small portions of the page without the server returning the full page again. Now, we have the ability to send data as JSON and combine that with HTML templates on the client side. This improves user experience by making the site react faster and reducing requests to the server.

One Language

Write both the client and the server parts of your interface in JavaScript.

—docs.meteor.com

JavaScript is the *de facto* language of the Internet. Web servers and server side frameworks are written in many different languages but client side programs are (almost) exclusively JavaScript. This means if you develop an app using a framework written in a language other than JavaScript, you have to learn that language and JavaScript. Switching languages adds an additional cognitive load that is difficult to manage for both beginners and seasoned developers. The solution is simple, use JavaScript for both the client and server.

Database Everywhere

Use the same transparent API to access your database from the client or the server.

—docs.meteor.com

Language switching isn't the only type of context switching that can slow development. Making database access the same in all parts of your app can both simplify your app and speed up development.

Latency Compensation

On the client, use prefetching and model simulation to make it look like you have a zero-latency connection to the database.

—docs.meteor.com

The web has grown from serving simple documents to being a platform capable of creating full applications. People expect applications to respond quickly, though. When dealing with any kind of remote connection there will be some latency. Luckily, Meteor keeps things as similar as possible on the client and server. So with latency compensation we can pretend like things happen instantly and correct as needed. Think of it like "trust, but verify".

Full Stack Reactivity

Make realtime the default. All layers, from database to template, should make an event-driven interface available.

—docs.meteor.com

In most frameworks a lot of time is spent making sure your data gets to the right spot. If something changes in the database then go to the view for that data and update it there, too. This is a lot to keep track of. Reactivity makes things simple. If you have a username, for example, and it changes in the database, it changes everywhere, in realtime. As soon as the username is changed, any browser viewing that username will be updated with the new value.

Embrace the Ecosystem

Meteor is open source and integrates, rather than replaces, existing open source tools and frameworks.

—docs.meteor.com

Instead of reinventing the wheel, Meteor brings together other open source projects and adds some shine. Why build your own Node.js when you could just use Node.js. Not only does this save on development, it also helps developers become instantly familiar with Meteor.

Simplicity Equals Productivity

The best way to make something seem simple is to have it actually be simple. Accomplish this through clean, classically beautiful APIs.

—docs.meteor.com

Meteor is a powerful web framework. But power and features alone won't make it useful. To truly be useful it must also be simple to use. Keeping Meteor simple means you can get more done faster, with less stress. Simplicity makes programmers happy.

Installing on Mac and Linux

Currently Meteor is only officially supported on Mac and Linux. Workarounds do exist for Windows and official Windows support is on the roadmap.

Just like most things with Meteor, the install is very simple. On all supported platforms the install is a single line. Through the rest of the book we will use Nitrous.io as our development environment since it is available on all platforms. Nitrous.io does not require Meteor to be installed on your local machine.

Meteor

Both Mac and Linux provide a terminal app that you can use to run commands for your system. To install Meteor locally, you simply run the following command (everything after the prompt '>') in your terminal.

```
> curl https://install.meteor.com | /bin/sh
```

That single line will setup everything you need to get started.

Atmosphere and Meteorite

Meteor comes with a group of official core packages that cover things that the majority of apps will need, like authentication. In addition to the core packages, the Meteor community has put together a repository of community-built packages called Atmosphere and can be found at http://atmospherejs.com. To install and manage packages from Atmosphere you use a tool called meteorite. Meteorite wraps the normal meteor command and adds the ability to install Atmosphere packages.

Meteorite is a node package so you can install it with a single command as well.

```
> npm install -g meteorite
```

Even though Meteor makes it really simple to develop on your local machine nothing is as simple as having a clean fresh environment all ready to go. That is what you get with Nitrous.io.

Developing in a Browser with Nitrous.io

What if you use an unsupported platform like a Chromebook or Windows computer? Well, don't fret! Nitrous.io comes to the rescue by providing a full Linux-based development environment in the cloud and accessible from your browser (Figure 2-1). In this chapter we will cover how you can use Nitrous.io to develop Meteor apps from any device that has a modern web browser.

A full-featured IDE in your browser

Code a variety of languages including Ruby, Python, Go, NodeJS and PHP. Run web servers, databases, caches and more right from the menubar.

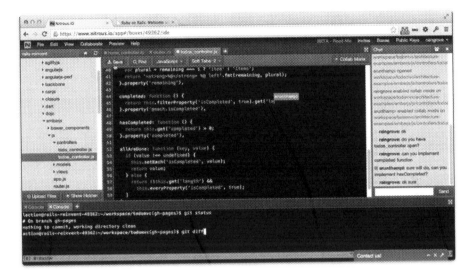

Figure 2-1. *The Nitrous.io web inter*

Create a Nitrous.io Account

To get started using Nitrous.io we need to sign up for an account. This can be done for free on http://nitrous.io with either the normal email and password sign up, or using an account from another service such as GitHub, Google, or LinkedIn (Figure 2-2).

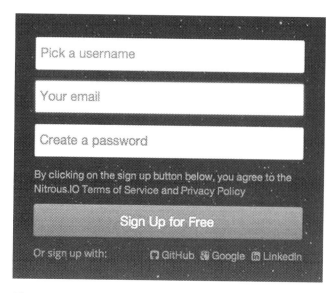

Figure 2-2. *Signing up for Nitrous.io*

Once your account is successfully created, go to the dashboard to see a list of Boxes on your account.

Setup a New Box

Nitrous.io works by setting up a preconfigured virtual Linux-based development environment that runs in the cloud. Each box is a self-contained Linux computer accessible through a web interface. To create a box, you click "New Box" form the "Boxes" section of the Nitrous.io Dashboard, as shown in Figure 2-3.

Figure 2-3. *Creating a new box*

This will open a simple box-creation page where you can select a template for the type of development you plan on doing, name your box, and assign the amount of resources available (Figure 2-4). Since Meteor.js is based on Node.js we will use the Node.js template. N2O is the Nitrous.io currency for giving your box different amounts of memory and storage. The free accounts include enough N2O to build a small, but adequate development box. Make sure you use your N2O to increase the amount of storage. You can add more N2O to your free account by doing things like inviting friends, or you can upgrade to a paid plan.

Figure 2-4. *Configuring your new box*

Once your box is provisioned, you will be automatically taken to the Integrated Development Environment (IDE) for that Box. Since each box is self-contained, you can have multiple boxes setup for different purposes, each with their own IDE and environment.

The Nitrous.io IDE

The main advantage of Nitrous.io is that you can access its full IDE through any modern browser. The Nitrous.io IDE lets you view and edit files, run commands on the command line, install additional packages, and collaborate with others (Figure 2-5).

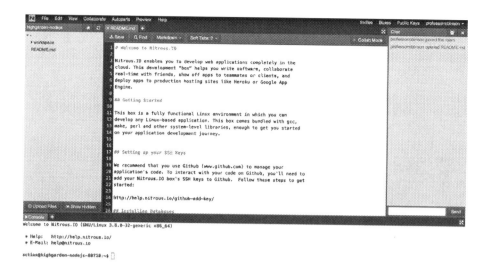

Figure 2-5. *The Nitrous.io web based Integrated Development Invironment (IDE)*

File Management

The left side of the IDE is used for file management (Figure 2-6). Nitrous.io starts out with a workspace directory and README.md file. The workspace directory is where you will keep all of your projects. Here we are showing the workspace with the example leaderboard app that you will create later. The README.md contains a good introduction to working with Nitrous.io.

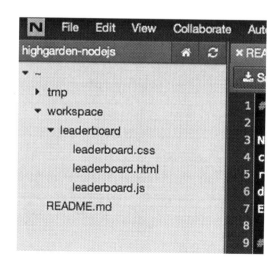

Figure 2-6. *File Management area of Nitrous.io with example leaderboard app*

The Editor

Developers can be passionate about the editor they use. While the Nitrous.io editor may not be as advanced as Vim, Emacs, Sublime Text, or others, it is very capable and has some handy features. When you first go to the Nitrous.io IDE, the editor is center stage filling the majority of the screen. It has syntax highlighting, file type detection, and a handy collab mode. Using the tabs across the top you can even edit multiple files at once (Figure 2-7).

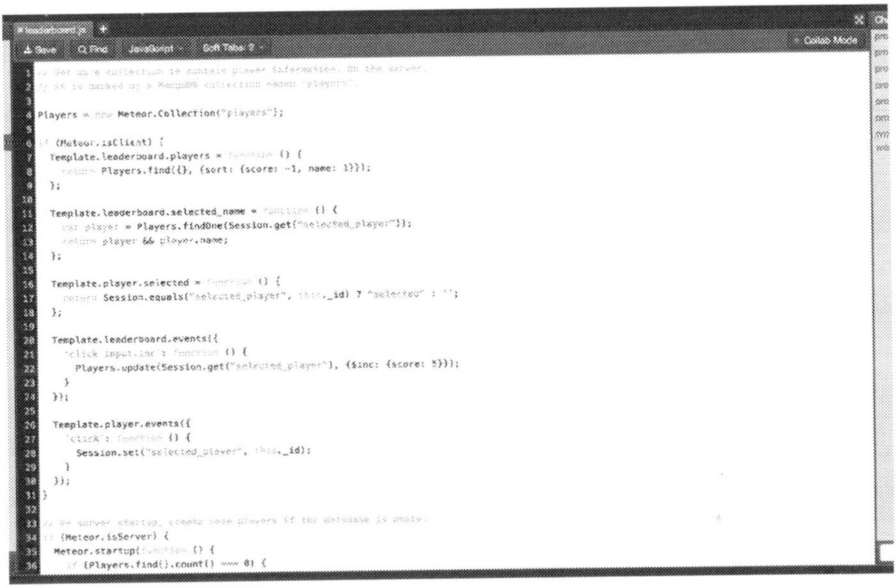

Figure 2-7. *Nitrous.io web based code editor*

The Console

Stretching across the bottom of the Nitrous.io IDE is the console (Figure 2-8). Since a Nitrous.io box is a full Linux virtual box running in the cloud, the IDE includes a real Linux console that we can use to install Meteor packages, start the server, or run any other Linux type commands. At this time, Nitrous.io doesn't allow root access but has a package manager, called Autoparts, which allows you to install packages that may normally need root access. Just like the editor, you can use the tabs across the top to run multiple console commands at once.

Figure 2-8. Nitrous.io web based console connected to the remote virtual machine

Collab Mode and Chat

One especially useful feature of the Nitrous.io IDE that isn't present in most other IDEs is collab mode. This feature is available on the right side of the IDE and allows you to invite other Nitrous.io users to work with you on a project. The chat section includes a log of what collaborators are doing, and lets you send messages to the group (Figure 2-9). When multiple people are editing the same file, and collab mode is enabled for that file, they will be able to see each other's cursor and changes in real-time.

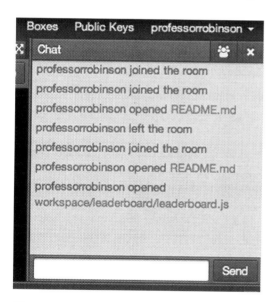

Figure 2-9. Nitrous.io chat window used to collaborate with others on development

Installing Meteor

Nitrous.io has a built-in package manager that makes installing Meteor a breeze. From the top of the IDE, just select Autoparts ➤ Manage Packages, as shown in Figure 2-10.

Figure 2-10. *Nitrous.io package manager named Autoparts*

When the package manager opens, search for the most recent Meteor package and click install, as shown in Figure 2-11.

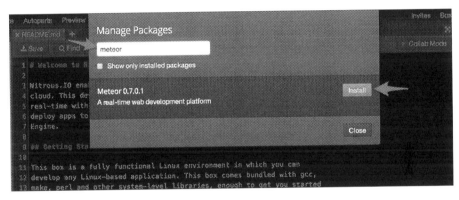

Figure 2-11. *Searching for a package in the Nitrous.io package manager*

Installing Meteorite

If you want to use packages from Atmosphere with Meteor you will need to install Meteorite as well. The Meteorite install works the same as on other platforms, and is installed using the Nitrous.io Console (Figure 2-12).

Figure 2-12. *Using the Nitrous.io console to install Meteorite*

Creating your First Meteor App

Now that you have your development environment all ready to go, it is time to create your first Meteor app. To start out, you will want make sure you have a folder where you can store all of your awesome new Meteor apps. If you are using Nitrous.io then a workspace folder will already be setup for you. Just make sure you are in the right directory by using the cd command in your console to change into your workspace.

```
$ cd ~/workspace
```

Once in your workspace you can use meteor create to create a new project.

```
$ cd ~/workspace
$ meteor create my-app
```

This will create a new folder called "my-app" that contains a bare bones Meteor app with just three files.

```
$ cd ~/workspace/my-app
$ ls
my-app.css    my-app.html    my-app.js
```

Running your Meteor App

Your new app may be bare bones, but it is enough to run. The Meteor server is run in the console from your projects directory.

```
$ cd ~/workspace/my-app
$ meteor
```

This will start a server running on port 3000 and viewable at http://localhost:3000. To use a port other than 3000 you can use the -p option when running the Meteor server.

```
$ meteor -p 4000
```

If you are using Nitrous.io then you won't be able to view your new app at http://localhost:3000, even though the console tells you otherwise. The reason is that localhost refers to your local computer but Nitrous.io is running Meteor in the cloud, and not on your local computer. Instead of going to http://localhost:3000 you need to use Preview ➤ Port 3000 from the Nitrous.io IDE (Figure 2-13), which will open a new browser tab where you can view your Meteor app.

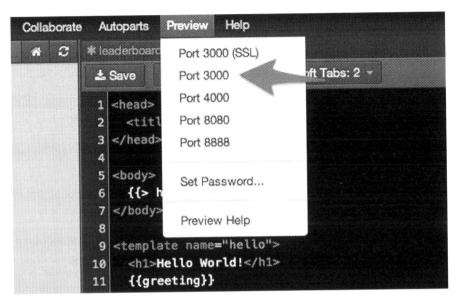

Figure 2-13. Selecting the port to preview your app using Nitrous.io

Example Apps

To get you started, Meteor comes with some example apps that can be generated with the meteor create command. Using the --example option followed by the example name will create a new project with the example code all loaded and ready to be explored.

```
$ cd ~/workspace
$ meteor create --example leaderboard
```

At the time of writing, the following examples are available:

- leaderboard
- parties
- todos
- wordplay

More information on the examples can be found at https://www.meteor.com/examples.

Getting to know the App Structure

Meteor is very flexible in how you structure your app. In general, you can organize it however you want, with the exception of a few special folders, and Meteor will figure it out. When you first create an app it will only consist of three files, one file each for HTML, CSS, and JavaScript.

The Public and Private Subdirectories

Just like most web frameworks and servers, the public folder is special in Meteor. It is where you store all your static client assets. Meteor doesn't do anything magical with the content of this subdirectory; all files are simply served at the root. This is where you will put things like images to make them available to your app.

The private subdirectory is the server equivalent of the public directory and is for static server assets. Meteor doesn't serve the content of this folder and makes it available to the server via the Assets API. This is the place to put data files you want to be only accessible to the server.

The Client, Server, and Test Subdirectories

HTML and CSS are only used on the client. Since JavaScript is used on both the client and server, though, we need a way to tell Meteor which files should be loaded on the client, and which should be loaded on the server. As expected, files put in the client subdirectory are only loaded on the client, and files put in the server subdirectory are only loaded on the server. So what about the test subdirectory? It isn't loaded anywhere since your test should be run outside of your app.

Compatibility Subdirectory

Meteor normally wraps each JavaScript file in a separate variable scope to keep them from polluting the global scope. This is normally what you want, but if a library breaks because it needs or expects to modify the global scope, then you can put it in client/compatibility. When files in this directory define a top-level variable, it will be in the global scope. Files in client/compatibility will also be run before other client-side JavaScript files.

Everything Else

Outside those magic directories, JavaScript files will be run on both the client and the server. Sometimes you may want some code to be available to both client and server, but only run on one or the other. To make this easy, Meteor provides a `Meteor.isClient` and a `Meteor.isServer` method, which returns a Boolean depending on where it is run.

Load Order

In most cases, the order files are loaded in shouldn't matter. However, when debugging odd issues knowing the order Meteor loads files can be helpful. Here are the basic rules Meteor uses when loading files:

1. Subdirectories are loaded first.

2. In each directory, files are loaded in alphabetical order.

3. Files in lib directories are loaded ahead of others.

4. Files matching main.* are loaded last.

Summary

In this chapter, we learned about the guiding principles of Meteor and what makes it different from other frameworks. We setup our development environments using officially supported platforms, and went over how to use Nitrous.io to develop Meteor apps anywhere we have access to a modern browser. Most importantly we created and ran our first Meteor app.

CHAPTER 3

Using Spacebars Templates

Now that we have Meteor and our development environment all setup, it is time to introduce Clans.io, the app we will be building together through the rest of this book. Clans.io is a micro social network for creating online communities. To do so, we'll need to learn about Spacebars, Meteor's template language, which will be used to create dynamic templates. We will then look at handling events and adding helpers to the template component object. Finally we'll use the Twitter Bootstrap package to add a simple nav bar to our app.

Creating the clans.io app

To get going, we will need a new app where we can play with templates. In this section, we are going to create a new app and take a look at the default template that Meteor gives you. From there, we will take a look at what the template is doing and what the components of a template are.

Let's start by changing into our workspace directory and creating the clans.io app.

```
$ cd ~/workspace
$ meteor create clans.io
```

Now, let's cd into our new apps folder.

```
$ cd clans.io
```

Our freshly minted Meteor app contains the standard three files. Let's start out by looking at clans.io.html.

```
<head>
  <title>clans.io</title>
</head>

<body>
  <h1>Welcome to Meteor!</h1>

  {{> hello}}
</body>
```

```
<template name="hello">
  <button>Click Me</button>
  <p>You've pressed the button {{counter}} times.</p>
</template>
```

This looks almost like normal HTML except that it has double curly braces, {{ and }}, all over the place. Those double curly braces are where the magic happens and are part of the Spacebars templating language that is part of Meteor.

Spacebars

Spacebars is inspired by Handlebars (http://handlebarsjs.com). Spacebars syntax is very similar to Handlebars, however it has been designed to support reactivity. Reactivity is the ability for the template to automatically detect, and reflect, changes in the underlying data.

Tags

The double curly braces delineate Spacebars tags. These tags turn your normal static HTML into powerful, dynamic, reactive, HTML templates.

In clans.io.html we see two of the major types of tags.

```
<body>
  <h1>Welcome to Meteor!</h1>

  {{> hello}}
</body>

<template name="hello">
  <button>Click Me</button>
  <p>You've pressed the button {{counter}} times.</p>
</template>
```

When you want to insert a string of text or a number you use double curly braces around the variable name that contains the string you want to insert. In our clans.io.html file we can see it used with "counter".

```
<template name="hello">
  <button>Click Me</button>
  <p>You've pressed the button {{counter}} times.</p>
</template>
```

A nice feature of the double curly braces is that it sanitizes your string and makes sure it doesn't add any unwanted HTML tags. This way, you can display user-supplied content without worrying about malicious tags being added to your page.

If you need to display the non-sanitized, and unsafe, contents of a variable, you can replace the double curly braces with triple curly braces.

```
<template name="hello">
  <button>Click Me</button>
  <p>You've pressed the button {{{counter}}} times.</p>
</template>
```

You may have noticed that wrapped around our counter is a template tag. This is an HTML5 tag that Meteor uses to define reusable pieces of HTML. The template tag's name attribute is used to give you a way to refer to your template.

Templates on their own are not displayed. To make your template visible, it must be include somewhere. That is done with the inclusion tag denoted by your usual double curly braces with the addition of a ">" followed by the template name. An example is in the body tag of your clans.io.html file.

```
<body>
  {{> hello}}
</body>
```

If the button is clicked 5 times, then clans.io.html would render to the following HTML:

```
<body>
  <h1>Hello World!</h1>
  <button>Click Me</button>
  <p>You've pressed the button 5 times.</p>
</body>
```

Using block tags like #each we can even iterate over a list of items and render a block of HTML for each item.

Here is what that would look like:

```
<ul>
  {{#each users}}
    <li>{{name}}</i>
  {{/each}}
</ul>
```

Now that we have an idea of what the boilerplate HTML file includes, let's dive into some of the details of Spacebars covered in the Spacebars package readme.

Identifiers

The variable inside a curly braced tag is actually a little more than a simple variable. It is called an identifier, and can be a value or a function. Spacebars looks for the identifier in the template helpers first, and if it can't find it there then it looks for a property on the current data context. Block tags usually set the data context.

```
<ul>
  {{#each users}}
    <li>{{name}}</i>
  {{/each}}
</ul>
```

Here, the #each block tag is setting the context to each user in turn before running the code inside the block. If we have an array of user objects like this:

```
[
  {
    name: "Andraya Ivy Robinson"
  },
  {
    name: "Leana Phi-Rose Robinson"
  }
]
```

Our block tag would give us:

```
<ul>
  <li>Andraya Ivy Robinson</li>
  <li>Leana Phi-Rose Robinson</li>
</ul>
```

Unlike the data context, which changes in block tags, the template helpers are defined per template. This is usually done in a corresponding JavaScript file.

```
<template name="hello">
  <h1>Hello World!</h1>
  <button>Click Me</button>
  <p>You've pressed the button {{counter}} times.</p>
</template>
```

In clans.io.html "counter" is the identifier and refers to a template helper function that we will take a look at later.

Helper Arguments

Since helpers are functions, you will probably want to send them some arguments from time to time. The arguments can be an identifier, a string, Boolean, number literal, or null. They are passed to the function inside the curly braces as a space-separated list.

```
{{ greeting "world" }}
```

This will call the greeting template helper with "world" as its first argument. Although Spacebars is executing your helper function here, it is important to remember that it does not execute arbitrary JavaScript.

Inclusion and Block Arguments

Inclusion tags and block tags can take at most one argument. You can pass in keyword arguments that will be turned into a data object.

Keyword arguments are passed inside of the curly braces as a space-separated list of key=value pairs:

```
{{#with x=1 y=2}}
  Value is {{x}}
{{/with}}
```

This will output:

```
Value is 1
```

Limitations

Spacebars is HTML-aware and works with the DOM. This means you can't put Spacebars tags anywhere you want, like you would with a string based templating system. Here are the main locations that they are allowed:

- At element level (i.e. anywhere an HTML tag could go)

- In an attribute value

- In a start tag in place of an attribute name/value pair

Double-braced Tags

The double-braced tag will evaluate to a string unless the identifier returns null, undefined, or false, in which case it will render nothing.

Since the double-braced tag escapes the value, you are not able to render HTML tags with it, unless you use SafeString.

SafeString

If you need to render HTML in a double-braced tag, you can override the default sanitization by returning a SafeString object instead of a string.

```
Spacebars.SafeString("<span>Some HTML</span>")
```

In this case the code calling SafeString is saying that it is ok to skip the normal sanitization and escaping processes.

In Attribute Values

Double-braced tags can be used in HTML attributes, which is very useful for setting classes.

```
<input type="checkbox" class="checky {{moreClasses}}" checked={{isChecked}}>
```

It is also smart enough to leave off an attribute if the indicator returns null, undefined, or false. This works well for checking a checkbox or marking a select option as selected. Keep in mind, though, that it will consider it present if anything else is returned, even an empty string.

Dynamic Attributes

If you aren't able to set the attributes how you want using attribute values, you can use a double-braced tag in an opening HTML tag to specify a whole set of attributes.

```
<div {{attrs}}>...</div>
```

Or

```
<input type=checkbox {{isChecked}}>
```

The identifier must evaluate to a string or an object with attribute names and the values as strings. A non-empty string should be an attribute name, and will be evaluated as an object with the string as its key and an empty string for the value. For example:

```
"checked"
```

Is the same as:

```
{"checked": ""}
```

If an empty string or null is returned, it is treated the same as an empty object.

Triple-braced Tags

Triple-braced tags are used for inserting raw HTML.

```
<template name="hello">
  {{{greeting}}}
  <button>Click Me</button>
  <p>You've pressed the button {{counter}} times.</p>
</template>
```

Since it is raw HTML, you cannot use the triple-braced tags for attributes. The HTML also needs to be fully formed and balanced. That means you can't use " " to close an existing tag and open a new one.

Inclusion Tags

The purpose of an inclusion tag is to insert the given template at the current location. Any argument given becomes the data context.

We can see an inclusion tag in our boilerplate clans.io.html file.

```
<body>
  {{> hello}}
</body>
```

Inclusion tags also let you set the data context for the template.

```
<body>
  {{> hello dataObject}}
</body>
```

So far we have only used the inclusion tags with a template name. However, you can use any identifier that evaluates to a template object, even a function.

Block Tags

It is best practice in any web framework to keep logic separate from the view. Spacebars helps with this by limiting what logic can be included in a template. Instead of allowing arbitrary JavaScript, we are limited to block tags.

```
{{#block}}
  <p>Hello</p>
{{/block}}
```

A block tag will invoke a built-in directive or custom block helper and pass it the block of template content that the block tag wraps.

To accommodate common control flow, block tags also allow for an else block.

```
{{#block}}
  <p>Hello</p>
{{else}}
  <p>Goodbye</p>
{{/block}}
```

As is the norm for Spacebars, the HTML passed in the block must be fully formed and balanced.

Block tags are also allowed in attribute values.

```
<div class="{{#if done}}done{{else}}notdone{{/if}}">
  <p>Hello World!</p>
</div>
```

If/Unless

The #if block tag is the same as most if statements. If the argument is true then it will render the block. When an else block is included it will be rendered when the #if block is false.

```
{{#if something}}
  <p>It's true</p>
{{else}}
  <p>It's false</p>
{{/if}}
```

Spacebars also includes an #unless block tag, which is the inverse of #if.

With

The #with block tag lets you set the data context of the enclosed block.

```
{{#with employee}}
  <div>Name: {{name}}</div>
  <div>Age: {{age}}</div>
{{/with}}
```

As we saw before, you can also use the object-specification format to set the exact values of the data context.

```
{{#with x=1 y=2}}
  This is {{x}}!
{{/with}}
```

You can also use #with as a form of #if tag, since it will not render the block if the argument is a falsy value. It even takes an optional else block.

Each

The #each block tag is extremely useful. It lets you iterate over a sequence that is passed in as an argument. It then renders the contents of the block using each value in the sequence as the context.

```
<ul>
  {{#each people}}
    <li>{{name}}</li>
  {{/each}}
</ul>
```

Custom Block Helpers

To create a custom block helper you can call a template with a block tag instead of an inclusion tag. This will give you access to the blocks in your template through:

```
{{> UI.contentBlock}}
```

And

```
{{> UI.elseBlock}}
```

For example, here is a helper used to wrap a block in a div.

```
<template name="note">
  <div class="note">
    {{> UI.contentBlock}}
  </div>
</template>
```

And it could be invoked with:

```
{{#note}}
  Any content here
{{/note}}
```

Comment Tags

Comment tags are good for leaving notes or seeing how something works with a bit of code disabled. A line comment is the usual double-brace but with an exclamation mark before your comment.

```
{{! Start of a section}}
<div class="section">
  <h1>Hello World!</h1>
</div>
```

If you want to block out a bigger chunk, you can use a "block comment".

```
{{!  This is a block comment.
     We can write {{foo}} and it doesn't matter. {{#with x}}
     This code is commented out.{{/with}} --}}
```

The syntax is similar to a line comment except that it adds "--".

Component Object

So far we have defined our templates in HTML using Spacebars.

```
<template name="hello">
  <button>Click Me</button>
  <p>You've pressed the button {{counter}} times.</p>
</template>
```

What we haven't looked at is the component object that Meteor automatically creates for us. We can see an example of the component object in the clans.io.js file that Meteor generated.

```
if (Meteor.isClient) {
  // counter starts at 0
  Session.setDefault('counter', 0);

  Template.hello.helpers({
    counter: function () {
      return Session.get('counter');
    }
  });

  Template.hello.events({
    'click button': function () {
      // increment the counter when button is clicked
      Session.set('counter', Session.get('counter') + 1);
    }
  });
}

if (Meteor.isServer) {
  Meteor.startup(function () {
    // code to run on server at startup
  });
}
```

The component object is accessible through the "Template" object, in the case of our "hello" template the component object is accessed through "Template.hello".

Events

To handle events on our template, we define an event map using the events method on the template's component object. This sounds more complex than it is. In clans.io.js we see a simple example of adding a "click" event handler to our "hello" template.

```
Template.hello.events({
  'click button': function () {
      // increment the counter when button is clicked
      Session.set('counter', Session.get('counter') + 1);   }
});
```

This event map adds an event handler to our "hello" template and watches for click events on button elements. Let's explore event maps in more detail and learn how to create our own.

Event Map

An event map is an object where the properties describe what events to watch for and the values provide a function to handle the events. In our clans.io.js file, the property was an event "click" followed by the element to watch, "input". The property can take one of a couple other formats.

```
// Event Only
"click": function(event, template) {
  if (typeof console !== 'undefined')
      console.log("You clicked");
}
```

If the property is set to just an event, the handler will be called any time that event is fired for the template. In our case, any time you click anywhere on the template you will get a console message.

```
// Event with selector
"click .clickable": function(event, template) {
  if (typeof console !== 'undefined')
      console.log("You clicked");
}
```

The selector follows the event after a space and can be any valid CSS selector. In the previous example, our handler will only fire when an element with the "clickable" class is clicked.

```
// Multiple Events
"click .clickable, click p": function(event, template) {
  if (typeof console !== 'undefined')
      console.log("You clicked");
}
```

You can add multiple events by separating them with a comma.

The handlers are passed two arguments to use when handling the event. The first is the event object, which gives you access to information about the event such as what element was clicked. This can be helpful since events bubble, and even though you are watching for a click on a <p> tag, it can be triggered by a click on any other tag inside the <p> tag.

```
// Event Object
"click": function(event, template) {
  if (typeof console !== 'undefined')
      console.log(event);
}
```

The second argument is a template instance, which gives you access to the template that the event was triggered in.

```
// Template Instance
"click": function(event, template) {
  if (typeof console !== 'undefined')
      console.log(template);
}
```

Inside the handler you also have access to the template's data context through "this".

```
// Template Data Context
"click": function(event, template) {
  if (typeof console !== 'undefined')
      console.log(this);
}
```

Returning false from a handler will both stop the event from bubbling, and prevent the default behavior.

Event Object

The function you set to handle an event will be passed an event object that gives you information about the event. It also provides several functions that can be used to control the event's propagation.

- type – String. What the type of the event is, such as "click" or "change".

- target – DOM Element. This returns the DOM element that the event was triggered on.

- currentTarget – DOM Element. This returns the DOM element that caught the event, and can be the same as the target. In the case of an event bubbling up, this will be the element that matched the selector.

- `which` – Number. Which tells you which mouse button was used to trigger a mouse event (1=left, 2=middle, 3=right) or which key was pressed for a key event.

- `stopPropagation()` – function. This will prevent the event from bubbling, or propagating, up to other elements. It will not prevent other events in this, or other, event maps from firing.

- `stopImmediatePropagation()` – function. This is prevents events from bubbling the same as `stopPropagation()`, but it also prevents events in this or other event maps from firing.

- `preventDefault()` – function. Prevents the action the browser would normally take in response to this event, such as following a link or submitting a form. Further handlers are still called, but cannot reverse the effect.

- `isPropagationStopped()` – function. Returns whether `stopPropagation()` has been called for this event.

- `isImmediatePropagationStopped()` – function. Returns whether `stopImmediatePropagation()` has been called for this event.

- `isDefaultPrevented()` – function. Returns whether `preventDefault()` has been called for this event.

Event Types

Event handlers and the event object all include an event type that describes the event. Some are obvious, like click or change, but some are a little less clear, like focus and blur.

- **click** – Mouse click on any element.

- **dblclick** – Double-click.

- **focus, blur (doesn't bubble)** – A text input field or other form control gains or loses focus.

- **change** – A checkbox or radio button changes state.

- **mouseenter, mouseleave (doesn't bubble)** – The pointer enters or leaves the bounds of an element.

- **mousedown, mouseup** – The mouse button is newly down or up.

- **keydown, keypress, keyup** – The user presses a keyboard key. `keypress` is most useful for catching typing in text fields, while `keydown` and `keyup` can be used for arrow keys or modifier keys.

Helpers

Each template component object contains helper functions that are accessible to the template. They are defined in two ways. We saw the first way in the generated clans.io.js:

```
Template.hello.helpers({
  counter: function () {
    return Session.get('counter');
  }
});
```

This passes an object to the "helpers" method. The second way simply defines the helper directly on the template's component object.

```
Template.hello.counter = function() {
    return Session.get('counter');
};
```

Using the "helpers" method is useful when adding a group of helpers at once.
To define a helper that can be accessed by every template, use UI.registerHelper.

```
UI.registerHelper("greeting", function () {
  return "Welcome to clans.io.";
});
```

onRendered

The onRendered method on the template component object lets you set a callback. The rendered callback is triggered when the template is initially rendered and inserted into the DOM for the first time.

```
Template.hello.onRendered(function() {
  if (typeof console !== 'undefined')
    console.log("Template rendered", this);
});
```

The template object is unique to this occurrence of the template, and will persist across re-renderings. It can be accessed inside of the callback using "this". Since the template has been rendered, you can use the template object to run any setup that requires the template to exist in the DOM.

```
Template.hello.OnRendered(function() {
  $(this.find('h1')).hide();
});
```

onCreated

Using the onCreated method on a templates component object adds a callback that is called before any template logic is evaluated.

```
Template.hello.onCreated(function() {
  if (typeof console !== 'undefined')
    console.log("Template created", this);
});
```

Inside the callback, this is the new template instance object. Properties you set on this object will be visible from the rendered and destroyed callbacks and from event handlers.

onDestroyed

The onDestroyed callback is called at the end of a template instance life cycle. It is called when a template instance is taken off the page for any reason and not re-rendered.

```
Template.hello.onDestroyed(function() {
  if (typeof console !== 'undefined')
    console.log("Template destroyed", this);
});
```

Inside the callback, this is the template instance object being destroyed. It fires once and is the last callback to fire.

Bootstrap Package

> *Twitter's Bootstrap package is a front-end toolkit for faster, more beautiful web development. Bootstrap provides simple and flexible HTML, CSS, and JavaScript for popular user interface components and interactions including typography, forms, buttons, tables, grids, and navigation.*

> —docs.meteor.com/#bootstrap

Now that we know how templates work, we are going to want to make them look good. Atmosphere provides a Twitter Bootstrap package that is automatically updated as newer Bootstrap versions are released.

```
> meteor add twbs:bootstrap
```

With this one line, we now have access to Twitter Bootstrap in our app. Let's try it out by making some changes to clans.io.html. Currently it looks like this:

```
<head>
  <title>clans.io</title>
</head>

<body>
  <h1>Welcome to Meteor!</h1>

  {{> hello}}
</body>

<template name="hello">
  <button>Click Me</button>
  <p>You've pressed the button {{counter}} times.</p>
</template>
```

Let's start by changing the "hello" template to "layout" and remove the default contents.

```
<body>
  {{> layout}}
</body>

<template name="layout">
</template>
```

Since we removed our "hello" template and replaced it with "layout" we are going to have to clean up our clans.io.js file as well.

```
if (Meteor.isClient) {
  Template.layout.events({
  });
}

if (Meteor.isServer) {
  Meteor.startup(function () {
    // code to run on server at startup
  });
}
```

Now let's add a nice responsive nav bar to our new layout template in clans.io.html.

```
<template name="layout">
  <div class="navbar navbar-inverse navbar-fixed-top" role="navigation">
    <div class="container-fluid">
      <div class="navbar-header">
```

```
    <button type="button" class="navbar-toggle" data-toggle="collapse"
    data-target=".navbar-collapse">
      <span class="sr-only">Toggle navigation</span>
      <span class="icon-bar"></span>
      <span class="icon-bar"></span>
      <span class="icon-bar"></span>
    </button>
    <a class="navbar-brand" href="#">Clans.io</a>
  </div>
  <div class="navbar-collapse collapse">
    <ul class="nav navbar-nav navbar-right">
      <li><a href="#">Help</a></li>
    </ul>
  </div>
  </div>
  </div>
</template>
```

It may not be much yet but we are starting to get something that resembles an actual app (Figure 3-1)!

Figure 3-1. *Simple app with a navbar*

Summary

In this chapter we got started on our app by using Meteor's template language, Spacebars, to create dynamic templates. We added a simple nav bar using the Twitter Bootstrap package, and now we can take our knowledge of event handling and helpers to build out the rest of our app.

■ ■ ■

CHAPTER 4

Reactive Programming and Routes

Now that you are able to handle basic interactions, let's cover a core concept of Meteor: reactive programming. This technique lets you write your code in a simple declarative style that enables your application to react to changes in the data. In its simplest form, this means you can tell your template to display something, such as a user's name, and when the data backing the name changes, the template automatically updates. Since this is such an important concept, this chapter will walk you through how to use reactive programming in your application.

Reactive Programming Explained

Reactivity is a programming concept that lets us monitor and respond to how data changes over time. It is an important aspect of – and largely what defines – realtime web applications.

A simple and elegant example of reactivity is the standard spreadsheet. When you tell cell C that it should equal the sum of cell A and cell B, then cell C will change anytime the values of cell A or cell B change. To make this happen, one simply declares that C = A + B and this simple computation for cell C reruns anytime its dependencies, A or B, change.

In a web application, this technique can be used to set the context of a current chat session with a specific user, display the current value of a single Bitcoin, or notify users of other users' online status.

Historically, such features required lots of custom AJAX (Asynchronous JavaScript and XML) and state logic to work well, which typically resulted in lots of unmaintainable code and underperforming applications. With the rise of the realtime web, lead largely by social media sites that include realtime notifications and web based tools that require realtime collaboration, users are starting to expect this functionality for a certain classification of apps. Meteor provides it right out of the box. In this chapter, we'll explore how Meteor makes the realtime web a default design pattern.

The Session Variable

The Session is a global object where you may store key-value pairs as a reactive data source. A reactive data-source can be described as a storage unit that a computation in your application depends on. If a computation uses a reactive data source, then it will recompute every time something of interest in the reactive data-store changes.

You can set the value of any arbitrary key

```
Session.set('currentClan', 'Denver Code Club');
```

You can retrieve the value of that key

```
Session.get('currentClan');
// => Denver Code Club
```

A key may be set to any JSON-able object, including strings, JSON, a Date, etc.

```
Session.set('currentClan', {title: 'Denver Code Club', city: 'Denver'});
var clanTitle = Session.get('currentClan').title;
console.log(clanTitle);
=> 'Denver Code Club'
```

Session is more powerful than a variable, and important in Meteor because it's able to report changes to computations concerned with such events. When a computation depends on the value of a reactive data source, like the Session, it will rerun the computation as soon as the data in its Session dependency changes. For a computation to depend on a Session, it just needs to be used anywhere within said computation.

To create a computation, we can use Meteor's built in Tracker.autorun(), which takes a callback function as the only argument. If a reactive data-source like a Session is used anywhere in the argument, then it is noted as a dependency and watched for changes.

Define a computation that uses a Session variable:

```
Tracker.autorun(function() {
  console.log('The current clan is ' + Session.get('currentClan') + '!');
});
```

Set the Session variable by passing the key as the first argument and a string as the second argument.

```
Session.set('currentClan', 'Sass Hack'});
=> 'The current clan is Sass Hack!'
Session.set('currentClan', 'Sass Hack Denver');
=> 'The current clan is Sass Hack Denver!'
```

Because the autorun function depends on the Session variable, currentClan, it will automatically run every time the value of currentClan changes.

Custom Reactivity

A computation will not rerun when a normal variable changes. When you need to respond to changes from something other than a Session variable, you can define your own custom, reactive data source with the Tracker object.

Under the hood, the Session actually uses Tracker to monitor and recompute computations as needed. Here's how we might use Tracker to define our own reactivity.

Create the variable of interest and create a new Tracker.Dependency

```
var currentClan = {title: 'Refresh Denver', city: 'Denver'};
var clanDependency = new Tracker.Dependency;
```

Notify our Tracker object that this function has dependencies.

```
var getClan = function () {
  clanDependency.depend();
  return currentClan;
}
```

Notify our Tracker object that its dependency has changed.

```
var setClan = function (clanObj) {
  currentClan = clanObj;
  clanDependency.changed();
}
```

Tell Tracker to autorun anytime the value of clan, a reactive data-source, changes.

```
Tracker.autorun(function() {
  var clan = getClan();
  console.log('Clan changed to ' + clan.title + '!');
});
```

Change the clan value using the setClan function.

```
setClan({title: 'Denver Gofers'});
=> 'Clan changed to Denver Gofers!'
```

Between the convenient Session variable and the flexible Tracker object, Meteor provides reactivity with relatively little effort and very little code.

House Cleaning

It's great that Meteor provides some default templates to get up and running, but in order to really start building out an application, you'll need to remove the default files and start building your own.

At the command line in the root of your project, delete all of the default templates made by meteor create.

```
$ rm clans.io.html clans.io.css clans.io.js
```

Create a new template in clans.io/client/views/clans/clans.html.

```
$ mkdir client/views
$ touch client/views/home/home.html
$ touch client/views/clans/clans.html
$ touch client/views/clans/clans.js
$ touch client/app.html
```

Open the new home.html file and define a template.

```
<template name="home">
        <h1>Clans.io</h1>
</template>
```

Create the clans template in client/views/clans/clans.html.

```
<template name="clans">
  This is where we will list all Clans.
</template>
```

Add standard HTML wrapper in client/app.html.

```
<head>
  <title>My App</title>
</head>
<body>
</body>
```

These templates provide the foundation for our application, but require major surgery to be of any use. Fortunately, the code required to proceed has been made available through a handful of community built Smart Packages.

Quick Intro to Packages

Packages are useful, built-in and third-party libraries of code designed specifically to enhance Meteor applications. There are currently 2,592 packages available on Atmosphere (atmospherejs.com), Meteor's official package catalog.

Install Packages

Meteor provides a few of useful commands to manage packages.

- **meteor add 272103_1_En:<package>** – This command checks Atmosphere for the specified package and installs it in your application. You tell it what package to get by giving it the author's name and package title separated by a colon.

- **meteor remove 272103_1_En:<package>** – This command checks for the specified package within your application and removes it entirely. The author and package title are also used as arguments to specify which package to remove.

Navigate to the root of your application (Figure 4-1) and install the Iron Router package.

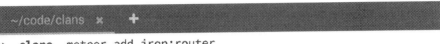

```
~/code/clans  ✕  +

→  clans   meteor add iron:router

iron:router: Routing specifically designed for Meteor
→  clans  ▊
```

Figure 4-1. *Adding a Meteor package*

In the background, Meteor finds the author 'iron' on Atmosphere, locates that author's package 'router', downloads it, installs it in your app, and adds it to your package manifest file in ~/workspace/clans.io/.meteor/packages, as seen in Figure 4-2. Then select "Show Hidden."

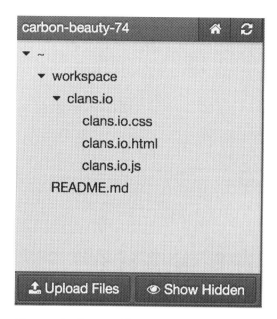

Figure 4-2. *Show Hidden option in the Nitrous.io filelist*

Now open up .meteor and view the packages file as shown in Figure 4-3. This is how Meteor keeps track of what packages are installed in your application.

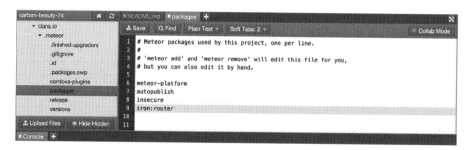

Figure 4-3. *Packages list inside the hidden .meteor folder*

In addition to the Iron Router package, a few of the Meteor core packages are included by default.

Add the Twitter Bootstrap package

Before we proceed to use Iron Router, let's install a package that will help make our application more presentable.

Add Bootstrap to your application

```
meteor add twbs:bootstrap
```

With that in place, you may start adding Bootstrap classes to your application. We'll make the most of Bootstrap shortly, but you will immediately notice that your site fonts and colors now have a prettier default.

Routes

The concept of routes refers to available URLs within your application. A router lets you define the context of your application based on a specific URL; it lets you define the available templates and available data depending on where your user is in your application. For instance, the homepage route, localhost:3000/, will use a specific homepage template; however, localhost:3000/clans will use a different template that displays all of the clans in your application.

Reactive Routes and Iron Router

Reactivity becomes immediately useful when we want to display different information for the different states of our application, based on where the user has navigated to. Consider that we will have a list of Clans and the user selects a single Clan to visit. Once the user selects a Clan, you may want to change the page title to that of the current clan without reloading the page or changing much of the HTML. If our Session variable is set when the user selects a specific clan, then you may use that Session data in your templates to dynamically display new data.

Meteor wants the server and the client to know about the routes you define in your application, so you write routing code in /both/router/routes.js, as any code placed in the 'both' folder will be run on the client and the server.

Router Defaults

Iron Router provides a convenient way for you to configure settings that apply to the entire application, such as what template to display while the app is in a loading state, or what template to show if the user types in a URL that doesn't exist.

Setup defaults for your entire application in /both/router/routes.js.

```
Router.configure({
  layoutTemplate: 'MasterLayout',
  loadingTemplate: 'Loading',
  notFoundTemplate: 'NotFound',
  templateNameConverter: 'upperCamelCase',
  routeControllerNameConverter: 'upperCamelCase'
});
```

Each option above has default settings and can be extended however you'd like.

layoutTemplate

This tells Iron Router what template you want to wrap all other templates inside of. Clans.io will use this for the persistent navigation, footer, and sidebar.

Create a new template in `client/views/layout/lmaster_layout.html`.

```
<template name="MasterLayout">
  <section class="container">
    {{> yield}}
  </section>
</template>
```

The yield helper comes with Iron Router and tells your application that, at any given route, there exists a template that should be inserted into that location.

loadingTemplate

This tells Iron Router what template you want to use when your application is in a loading state. This will become useful for the initial page load and any time your app makes a large request to the server.

Create a new template in `client/views/shared/loading.html`.

```
<template name="loading">
        <h1>Loading...</h1>
</template>
```

notFoundTemplate

This tells Iron Router what template to use when the user navigates to a URL that is not defined and thus does not exist.

Create a new template in `client/views/shared/not_found.html`.

```
<template name="not_found">
        <h1>Oops! This page doesn't exist</h1>
</template>
```

templateNameConverter

This tells Iron Router that you will use a specific syntax – different than what you write to declare routes – when you name your templates.

routeControllerNameConverter

This tells Iron Router that you will use a specific syntax to name your application controllers.

First Route

To define a route, you need to provide it as an argument to Iron Router's map function.

First custom route for the homepage.

```
Router.map(function () {
  this.route('home', {path: '/'});
});
```

This tells Iron Router that it should provide the home template when the user navigates to the '/', or root, URL, which in our case, is localhost:3000. To add more routes, you simply declare them within this map.

First custom route.

```
Router.map(function () {
  this.route('home', {path: '/'});
  this.route('clans', {path: '/clans'});
});
```

Create a new template in client/views/clans/clan.html.

```
<template name="clans">
  <h1>Clans</h1>
</template>
```

With this template and the clans route defined, you may now navigate to the new template by visiting localhost:3000/clans. However, you can't expect users to navigate this way, so now is a great time to include a navigation in the master layout.

Create a new template in client/views/layout/lmaster_layout.html.

```
<template name="MasterLayout">
  <section class="container">
    <ul class="nav nav-pills">
      <li><a href="{{pathFor 'home'}}" >Home</a></li>
      <li><a href="{{pathFor 'clans'}}" >Clans</a></li>
    </ul>
    {{> yield}}
  </section>
</template>
```

The pathFor helper comes with Iron Router and only needs the name of the routes defined in the router. Users may now navigate back and forth between the new templates in clans.io.

To show a list of clans in the clans template, we need to define a clans helper that returns an array of clans. This is fairly basic code that we'll improve upon using MongoDB in the next chapter.

Create clans helper for clans template.

```
Template.clans.helpers({
  clans: function () {
    return [
      {title: 'Sass Hack Denver'},
      {title: 'Denver Gophers'},
      {title: 'Boulder.rb'}
    ]
  }
});
```

Add Spacebars in clans template to iterate on data

```
<template name="clans">
  <h1>Clans</h1>
  {{#each clans}}
    <h2>{{title}}</h2>
  {{/each}}
</template>
```

Figure 4-4 shows the result from the clans template and helper data.

Home   Clans

Sass Hack Denver

Denver Gophers

Boulder.rb

Figure 4-4. *Result from the clans template and helper data*

Summary

In this chapter, we explored the depths of Meteor's reactive nature, learned how to use packages to aid development, defined custom routes for clans.io, created a few new templates, and made everything look pretty.

CHAPTER 5

Dealing with Data

Meteor does a wonderful job of making the syncing of client-side data, something traditionally difficult, very easy. It does this by providing a client-side implementation of MongoDB, called MiniMongo, which syncs with the backend database and pushes to other clients in realtime. This amazing feature is both simple to use and extremely powerful. This chapter will describe setting up Meteor collections and using them to pass data around an app.

Collections

In previous chapters, clans were included as an array of objects in memory to illustrate how basic reactivity works. This worked well for prototyping the clans view, but it's not a solution if we want our data to be stored and manipulated by users over time. Now you will define your first collection using MongoDB and MiniMongo (Listing 5-1).

Listing 5-1. Create first collection in both/collections/clan.js

```
Clan = new Mongo.Collection('clan');
```

Because this is added in the both folder, Meteor will make the database available to the client and the server, MiniMongo and MongoDB respectively. This one statement tells Meteor that your whole application will make use of a collection called Clan. You can now use query methods on this collection in other parts of the application. Now that this collection is defined, go to the clans view and replace the static array with a call to this collection.

```
Template.clans.helpers({
  clans: function () {
    return Clan.find();
  }
});
```

The return statement now makes a call to Mongo to grab every clan stored in the application. There aren't any clans now, so our clans view is empty. Let's fix that. Navigate to http://localhost:3000 in the browser and open up your browser's developer tools. In Chrome you can access the console with Command + Shift + J and in Firefox it's Command + Alt + K.

Inside the browser's console, insert the first clan as illustrated in Figure 5-1.

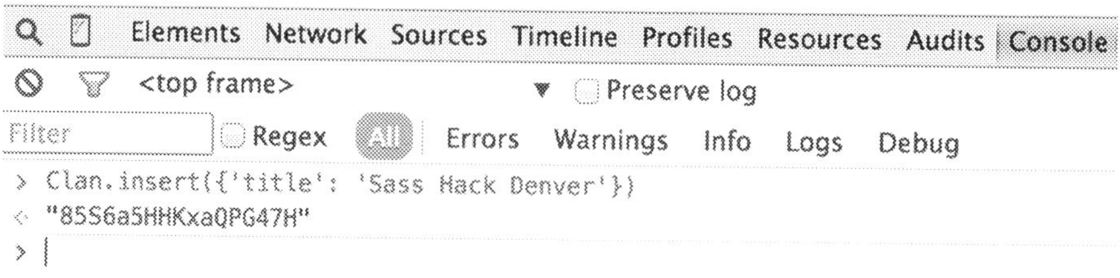

Figure 5-1. *Inserting a record with MiniMongo*

With just that statement, you should now see the first Clan reappear in the clans view. Notice how the new record was inserted into the page without refreshing the browser. Meteor managed to update the database and the view all at once.

When you call insert on a Meteor collection, you only need to pass an object that represents the document you want to store in Mongo. It then saves the document and returns the unique ID associated with it.

▓ **Note about Meteor security**   You're able to insert new documents from the browser console because this application currently has the default, "insecure" package included. This is really useful for prototyping and we will leave it in for now, but plan to remove this package before going live.

Database Reactivity

To demonstrate how Meteor pushes new documents to the browser from anywhere, open up a new terminal window to play with Mongo from the server.

```
meteor mongo
db.clan.insert({'title': 'Clan from the server'})
```

Even though the browser never sees this actual database insert, it still updates the browser without ever refreshing the page. This is accomplished by pairing Meteor's reactivity with a technology called web sockets. Meteor is able to create a realtime connection with MongoDB, which broadcasts the new data to Meteor's reactive templates.

MongoDB and NoSQL

MongoDB is the default database used within Meteor applications. Like Meteor, MongoDB is an open source technology that has raised capital to ensure its continued development.

Sometimes, MongoDB is described as a NoSQL database. To understand what that means, it helps to consider what an SQL-based database is. SQL-based databases, like PostgreSQL or MySQL, use a table structure which often facilitates relational data. These relational databases can be thought of much like a spreadsheet with multiple tabs, in that each type of data is stored with columns and rows. NoSQL, on the other hand, is non-relational database. A non-relational database uses a nested document structure to facilitate relationships.

Where in SQL we create two separate tables for Clans and Posts, in MongoDB we can nest Posts within a Clan, which implicitly defines them as belonging together.

Listing 5-2. Example MongoDB Document for a single Clan

```
{
  title: 'Sass Hack Denver',
  posts: {
    {
      title: 'Event Announcement',
      user: 'NaviRosland'
    },
    {
      title: 'SassConf! Who is going?',
      user: 'Adrian'
    }
  }
}
```

You may recognize this syntax as looking like JSON (JavaScript Object Notation). This is effectively how your data is stored, but unlike JSON, MongoDB provides unique query operations, or ways to access data, that plain JavaScript does not.

Mongo provides a handful of query methods that let developers easily manage data. The most common operations are often summarized with the CRUD acronym. It stands for Create, Read, Update, and Destroy.

Create

Using MiniMongo to create a new document in MongoDB you use the insert method. This is the same method we used to generate new documents from the terminal and console before.

```
Clan.insert({'title': 'New Clan Title!'})
```

This creates a new document in the Clan collection and returns a unique ID for that document.

Read

You can ask for all documents with the find method.

```
Clan.find()
```

This returns a cursor that represents all documents in the Clan collection.

To find only one document, the find method accepts an object with attributes that you want to match. For instance, to find a single document with the ID of '1234', you can do the following.

```
Clan.find({'id': '1234'})
```

Update

To update a document, you need to tell Mongo what document you want to update and specify a new document or the fields that need to be changed.

```
Clan.update({_id: "1234"}, {title: "Updated Title Value"});
```

Destroy

You can destroy a document with the destroy method. It requires an ID of the document you want to remove.

```
Clans.remove('1234')
```

How Meteor Handles Data

You can't expect users to create new data from the console and terminal, so now is a good time to introduce forms into the application. The vast majority of websites and web applications exist to gather and organize user input and largely do so through forms. A form is used anytime a visitor registers as a new user, posts a comment, or uploads an image.

aldeed:autoform

The Meteor community recognized the importance of forms, and through a Smart Package they have made it simple to capture user input and send data to Mongo on the server.

```
meteor add aldeed:autoform
```

This package makes it super easy to include forms that relate to any Meteor collection. Once it is installed, you need to tell it about the form fields you want it to help with. Next, we're going to install collection2, a package that allows you to attach a schema to a Mongo collection and automatically validate input against that schema when inserting and updating from client or server code.

```
meteor add aldeed:collection2
```

Now that collection2 is installed, reopen clan.js to define a schema.

```
Clan = new Mongo.Collection('clan');

Clan.attachSchema(
  new SimpleSchema({
    title: {
      type: String,
      label: "Title"
    }
}));
```

The collection2 package added an attachSchema method to all MongoDB collections. This allows you to define what fields you want associated with each document in the collection. To keep things simple, the above code defines only a title field. The type attribute tells Collection2 that this field will only accept strings and the label attribute tells Autoform what label to give the form field.

With that in place, you can easily generate new forms for this collection throughout the application using Autoform helpers.

Listing 5-3. In client/views/clans.html

```
{{> quickForm collection="Clan" id="clanBookForm" type="insert"}}
```

The quick form helper uses three attributes:

1. The collection attribute tells the helper what Mongo collection it should know about.

2. The id attribute is used internally in Autoform and must be unique across the entire application

3. The type attribute lets Autoform know if it should insert, remove, or update a given record.

This one line generates a form that inserts new clans at the clans route.

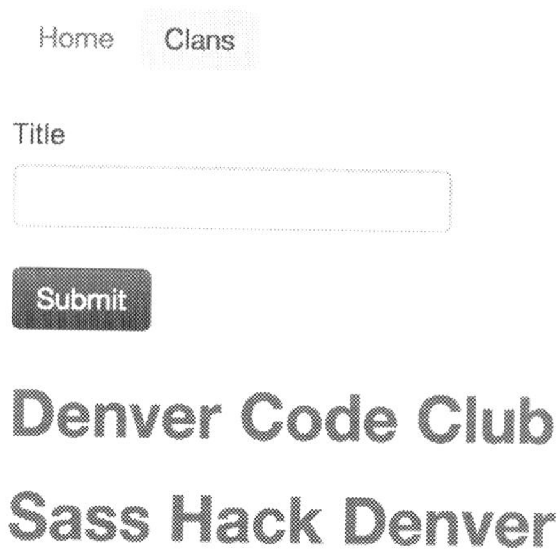

Home   Clans

Title

Submit

Denver Code Club
Sass Hack Denver

Figure 5-3. *Adding the clan view template*

Latency Compensation

When a user submits a form, deletes an item, or changes the title of a document, the new data must be validated on the server. In traditional web applications, the new data is sent to the server, validated there, and the appropriate response is sent back to the client. While this validation process happens, the user is left waiting.

Instead, Meteor assumes the new data is valid long enough to post it to MiniMongo in the client and render the updated view. Meanwhile, Meteor delegates validation to another process on the server and only returns an error – which we can handle appropriately – if something goes wrong. For this reason, latency compensation can be thought of as an optimistic way to build user interfaces. Unless the user provides invalid data, then the application feels abnormally fast.

Publish and Subscribe

By default, Meteor applications expose all of the data in MongoDB to all users at every route in your application. This is great for prototyping, but as your application goes to production and grows in size, it will become a performance and security concern, so it's a good idea to remove this functionality sooner rather than later.

```
meteor remove autopublish
```

After removing this package, you will notice that none of the Clans show up at the clans route. This is because autopublish implicitly sent clan data to that route and implicitly subscribed to said data. With autopublish removed, we need to explicitly set this up.

Listing 5-4. Create a publish function in clans.io/server/publish/clans.js

```
Meteor.publish('clans', function () {
  return Clan.find();
});
```

This publication is done from the server where we can access MongoDB directly and it simply checks the database for all clans with the find method. This publish function is defined once and can be called with a subscribe function from anywhere in the application.

Listing 5-5. Create a route controller for clans in clans.io/client/controllers/clans.js

```
ClansController = RouteController.extend({
  waitOn: function () {
    return Meteor.subscribe('clans');
  },

  data: function () {
    return Clan.find().fetch();
  }
});
```

This route controller above tells Iron Router that the clans route should wait for the subscribe method to complete before it returns the clans data to the clans route. Let's review this line by line.

```
ClansController = RouteController.extend
```

The ClansController is named such intentionally. This tells Iron Router that it belongs specifically to the clans route that is defined in the router. The RouteController object was previously using defaults that depend on the autopublish package to work. Since we removed the autopublish package, we need to use the extend method to reopen and redefine some of its default properties.

```
waitOn: function () {
    Meteor.subscribe('clans');
},
```

The waitOn method tells the application to prevent template rendering until the subscription has been satisfied. The subscribe method asks the server for publications named 'clans', waits for the clans publication to return data, and then moves onto the data method.

```
data: function () {
    return Clan.find().fetch();
}
```

The data method can now assume that any subscriptions have been satisfied, so the client officially has all of the clan data it needs. To make it available to the clans route, you just return data from the find method like we were previously doing before autopublish was removed.

Edit Clans

Users will need to edit the data for each clan they set up, so let's set that up now. The first step is to create a route for a single clan's show page.

Create a Route:

Listing 5-6. Add a route to both/router/router.js

```
this.route('clan', {path: '/clan/:id'});
```

Unlike other routes, this route includes the :id parameter. This is a variable value that tells Iron Router we expect the URL to include a unique value at that location in the URL.

There are a handful of ways to point the browser to the correct URL for a given clan. For now, you can hard code an anchor link around the title of each clan in the clans template.

Listing 5-7. Updated clans template in client/views/clans/clans.htmt

```
<template name="clans">
  {{> quickForm collection="Clan" id="clanBookForm" type="insert"}}
  {{#each clans}}
    <h2>
      <a href="/clan/{{_id}}">{{title}}</a>
    </h2>
  {{/each}}
</template>
```

The {{_id}} property will evaluate to the document id for each clan in the clans data, just like the title property evaluates to each clan's title.

Given the route definition added to the router above, recall that Iron Router assumes there is a new template based on the route's name. To provide that template, add the following to the application.

Listing 5-8. Add new template to client/views/clan/clan.html

```
<template name="Clan">
    <h1>{{title}}</h1>
</template>
```

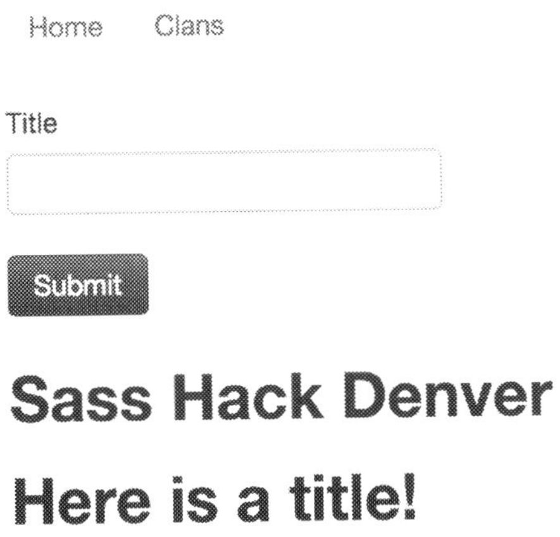

Home   Clans

Title

Submit

Sass Hack Denver

Here is a title!

Figure 5-2. Form to insert new record

The new route, links, and template get us close, but if you follow the links you may notice there is no data at the new route. Just like the clans route, the application needs to explicitly publish and subscribe data for the clan route.

Listing 5-9. Add a new publish method in server/publish/clans.js

```
Meteor.publish('clan', function (id) {
 return Clan.find(id);
});
```

Notice that this publish method takes an argument called id. The id's value will get passed into this function when we set up the subscribe method in a new route controller below.

Listing 5-10. Add new route controller in client/controllers/clan.js

```
ClanController = RouteController.extend({
  waitOn: function () {
    var id = this.params.id;
    return Meteor.subscribe('clan', id);
  },

  data: function () {
    var id = this.params.id;
    return Clan.findOne(id);
  }
});
```

Now that the publish and subscribe methods return data to the new clan route, the title will display at a given clan route as expected. Let's edit the clan template to include a form that lets users edit the title.

Listing 5-11. Add reactive variables and a quickform to client/views/clan/clan.html

```
<template name="Clan">
  {{#if isEditing}}
    <h1>Edit {{title}}</h1>
    {{> quickForm collection="Clan" doc=this id="updateClansForm"
    type="update"}}
  {{else}}
    <h1>{{title}}</h1>
    <button class="btn edit">Edit</button>
  {{/if}}
</template>
```

There are two parts to the clan template now. The isEditing boolean will be a reactive variable that toggles from false to true based on user interaction. When the variable is set to true, the quickform will display, otherwise everything inside of the else block will display instead.

Let's create some template helpers to enable users to toggle between the two states.

Listing 5-12. Add template helpers in client/views/clan/clan.js

```
Template.Clan.helpers({
  isEditing: function() {
    return Session.get('isEditing');
  }
});
```

The isEditing property returns the value of the reactive Session variable 'isEditing'. When the template first loads, this variable will be undefined, which is a falsy value for the HTMLBars template, so the template will default to showing everything defined in the 'else' block.

Below the template helpers in the same file, include template event handlers to capture when users click the edit button.

Listing 5-13. Template events in client/views/clan/clan.js

```
Template.Clan.events({
  'click .edit': function() {
    Session.set('isEditing', true);
  }
});
```

When the users click the edit button, the reactive variable is set to true and the clan template renders the edit form.

Autoform provides a handful of events for you to hook into. For now, we want to toggle the isEditing variable to false after a user saves changes to a given Clan.

```
AutoForm.addHooks('updateClansForm', {
  onSuccess: function () {
    Session.set('isEditing', false);
  }
});
```

The 'updateClansForm' should match the ID of the update form defined in the corresponding template. This lets us hook into the onSuccess event for that specific form.

Because Session creates global variables, it's a good idea to set it back to the default when the user leaves the clan route. Otherwise, the isEditing Session variable could remain 'true', which would render the edit form by default at other clan routes. To do that, you can respond to the destroyed hook on the clan template.

Listing 5-14. Add destroyed hook in client/views/clan/clan.js

```
Template.Clan.destroyed = function () {
  Session.set('isEditing', false);
};
```

Summary

In this chapter, we've explored how to create routes with variable parameters, publish and subscribe to data at specific routes, and build reactivity into application templates. Users should now be able to create, read and update the title of ever clan. Because the ability to delete data is a bit more involved, it is intentionally left out of this quick introduction to Meteor. In the next chapter, we'll wrap up our basic app and show you how to deploy it.

CHAPTER 6

Authentication and Deployment

Now that you understand how to create and edit Meteor templates, how to handle routing via Iron Router, and how to create, delete, and update a data model working on top of the default Meteor MongoDB backend, it's time to tie everything together and wrap up our Clans.io application.

In this final chapter, we will look at how to restructure our Meteor app so that it supports simple user authentication. For example, we will only allow logged-in users to create and join clans.

Prerequisite Packages

We will continue to leverage the Meteor ecosystem by installing a few packages that allow us to support user authentication essentially out-of-the-box. As you saw in Chapter 4, it's easy to add packages in Meteor using the `meteor add` command. At your console, type these three commands inside your project directory:

```
meteor add useraccounts:bootstrap
meteor add accounts-password
meteor add useraccounts:iron-routing
```

Let's now take a quick look over what those three packages will add to the application.

useraccounts:bootstrap

The first package, `useraccounts:bootstrap`, will enable your app to use pre-built Bootstrap-styled templates for sign-in pages, sign-up pages, password recovery pages, and several others. Keep in mind that even though these templates are very bare-bones, they can be fully customized and will work seamlessly with Meteor's `useraccounts:core`.

Keep in mind that `useraccounts:bootstrap` does not add any other packages providing Bootstrap. This is to let you choose the import and styling method that you prefer, so you can choose: compiled, LESS, SASS, or from a content delivery server.

accounts-password

The second packages, accounts-password is what Meteor calls an *account service*. Account services bridge the gap between the Meteor User object and some sort of external input that authenticates the user. In our case, the input will be an email and password, but we could potentially use a GitHub account service, a Facebook account service, an OAuth account service, and so on. Essentially, Meteor does its best to make it as easy as possible to support logging into your website or app with any external service as well as the "vanilla" accounts-password solution, which we will be using.

Note that user authentication, password strength requirements, and validation are all handled out-of-the-box, so we don't need to worry about any of those implementation details. Thanks, Meteor!

useraccounts:iron-routing

Finally, useraccounts:iron-routing is a package that will make sure that the templates provided by useraccounts:bootstrap will be reachable via an Iron Router route.

Before you can configure routes for User Accounts with Iron Router, you will need to make sure you have set a few configuration items. Assuming that you have a main layout that looks like Listing 6-1:

Listing 6-1. The main layout template

```
<template name="myLayout">
  {{> yield region='nav'}}

  <div id="content">
    {{> yield}}
  </div>

  {{> yield region='footer'}}
</template>
```

You will need to configure the Iron Router as shown in Listing 6-2:

Listing 6-2. The Iron Router configuration for the main layout template

```
Router.configure({
    layoutTemplate: 'masterLayout',
    yieldTemplates: {
        myNav: {to: 'nav'},
        myFooter: {to: 'footer'},
    }
});

AccountsTemplates.configure({
    defaultLayout: 'myLayout',
});
```

This will ensure that AccountTemplates will load the appropriate Bootstrap layouts in the right layout container. Keep in mind that you need to configure the Router **before** you define the routes.

Re-structuring the Application

Next, we need to slightly restructure the overall architecture of the app so that it will support user action based on the authentication status of a user; either logged in or not logged in. For example, if a user is logged in, she can join a clan or create a new clan. If a user is not logged in, he can make a new Clans.io account. First, we modify the /client/views/clan.html template, as shown in Listing 6-3:

Listing 6-3. The revised /client/views/clan.html template

```
<template name="clan">
  <div class="well">
    <h2>
      {{ name }}
      {{#if currentUser}}
      <a class="join btn btn-primary">Join</a>
      {{/if}}
    </h2>
    {{#unless currentUser}}
      <p>Login to Join this Clan.</p>
    {{/unless}}
    <h3>Members</h3>
    <div class="list-group">
      {{#each members}}
        <a class="list-group-item">{{ _id }}</a>
      {{/each}}
    </div>
  </div>
</template>
```

Joining a Clan

The first change here is that we no longer support editing a clan; instead, we output a list of the IDs of the members that are part of the clan. We also provide a "Join" button for logged-in users only. This is done within the {{#if currentUser}} block.

Here, currentUser is a template helper that simply returns Meteor.user() – that is, the currently logged in user, if any. If the user is not logged in, Meteor.user() (and therefore currentUser) will always return **null**. Make sure to always do a null check when using this object. If the user is not logged in, the template above simply prints

"Login to Join this Clan." The event attached to this button is in /client/views/clan.js, which should look like Listing 6-4:

Listing 6-4. The button event in the /client/views/clan.js file

```
Template.clan.events({
  "click .join": function (event) {
    event.preventDefault();

    Clans.update(this._id, {
      $push: { member_ids: Meteor.user()._id }
    });
  }
})
```

This snippet of code pushes the current user ID into the member_ids array of the Clan Mongo object, essentially making this user part of the respective clan. This is all that we need to do to make sure that when a logged-in user presses "Join", she joins the clan!

Getting a List of Clan Members

In our clan template, we iterate over what appears to be a members array. However, as we'll see, we never actually define this array in the model itself. Rather, we use a Meteor feature called a **transform**. The transform function, when in a collection object, will ensure that Mongo documents will be passed through this function before being returned from fetch or findOne, and before being passed to callbacks of observe, allow, and deny. To see the transform function in action, we can look at /lib/collections/clans.js, shown in Listing 6-5:

Listing 6-5. The transform function in /lib/collections/clans.js

```
Clans = new Mongo.Collection("clans", {
  transform: function(doc) {
    doc.members = Meteor.users.find(
              {_id: {$in: doc.member_ids || []}}
        );
    return doc;
  }
});
```

The above transform function ensures that the returned Mongo document will have a members property, which will either be an array of member_ids of members in the respective clan or, if no such members exist, an empty array. We need the optional empty array here so that we avoid doing null checks when trying to access the members array directly (for example, in the {{#each members}} block).

Creating and Listing Clans

To see how we create clans, we first need to take a look at /client/views/clans.html, as shown in Listing 6-6:

Listing 6-6. The clan generation code from /client/views/clans.html

```
<template name="clans">
  <div class="list-group">
    <header class="list-group-item">
      <form class="new-clan">
        <input class="form-control" type="text" name="text"
        placeholder="Type to add new clan" />
      </form>
    </header>
    {{#each clans}}
      <a class="list-group-item" href="{{pathFor route='clan.show' }}">
      {{ name }}</a>
    {{/each}}
  </div>
</template>
```

It's noteworthy to understand that the app allows clans to be created by anyone, even non-authenticated users. This is in contrast with the previous section, where to join a clan we needed to be authenticated. This is a purposeful omission. An app in the real world will need to have a feature set that might be available only to privileged users whereas some other feature may be available to all users. Similarly, Clans.io provides examples for both. This lack of authentication when creating new clans is perhaps more obvious when looking at /client/views/clans.js, as shown in Listing 6-7:

Listing 6-7. Our clans helper illustrating the lack of authentication required for this feature

```
Template.clans.helpers({
  clans: function () {
    return Clans.find({});
  }
})

Template.clans.events({
  "submit .new-clan": function (event) {
    event.preventDefault();

    var name = event.target.text.value;

    Clans.insert({
      name: name,
      member_ids: [],
      createdAt: new Date() // current time
    });
```

```
      event.target.text.value = "";
  }
})
```

Here, we have a clans helper that returns a list of all clans in the Mongo database; the clans helper is used in the template to iterate over all clans by calling {{#each clans}}. We also have a submit event that is handled by inserting a new clan in the database. Again, note how there is no authentication here. This functionality is available to all users – authenticated or otherwise.

The name of the clan, indicated by the name field, is assigned to the value of the textbox after the Return/Enter key is pressed and it is submitted. After the clan is created, the value of the textbox is reset, allowing the end-user to insert another clan.

Updated Templates

Okay, now that we've updated the code for creating, joining, and listing clans, let's turn our attention to our view templates. First, we define a new template that will serve as the "splash page" when a user first comes across our app. We create a new file as /client/views/home.html, shown in Listing 6-8:

Listing 6-8. The code for our new splash page

```
<template name="home">
  <div class="text-center well">
    <h3>Welcome to Clans</h3>
    <p>Pick a clan to join from the menu on the left or create your own.</p>
  </div>
</template>
```

This is a simple template consisting of only HTML. We'll call it **home**. Next, we'll slightly modify our master layout that we first created in Chapter 4 by adding navigation and content regions, as shown in Listing 6-9:

Listing 6-9. The revised master layout template in /views/layout/master_layout.html

```
<template name="masterLayout">
  {{> yield region='nav'}}
  <div id="content" class="master-layout">
    {{> yield}}
  </div>
</template>
```

It is also prudent to add a /client/main.html file, which will serve as the simple "blueprint" for all of our compiled templates. See Listing 6-10:

Listing 6-10. Our new blueprint template

```html
<head>
  <meta charset="utf-8">
  <title>Clans</title>
</head>

<body>
</body>
```

Having a main.html file makes sure that HTML metadata (like title or character set information) is consistent side-wide. This file is optional. Next, we'll need to define a navigation bar in /client/nav.html, shown in Listing 6-11:

Listing 6-11. The new navigation bar code

```html
<template name="nav">
  <nav class="navbar navbar-inverse navbar-static-top" role="navigation">
    <div class=container>
      <div class="container-fluid">
        <div class="navbar-header">
          <button type="button" class="navbar-toggle" data-toggle="collapse"
          data-target="#bs-example-navbar-collapse-8">
            <span class="sr-only">Toggle navigation</span>
            <span class="icon-bar"></span>
            <span class="icon-bar"></span>
            <span class="icon-bar"></span>
          </button>
          <span class="navbar-brand">
            Clans
          </span>
        </div>

        <div class="collapse navbar-collapse" id="bs-example-navbar-
        collapse-8">
          <ul class="nav navbar-nav navbar-right">
            {{> atNavButton}}
          </ul>
        </div>
      </div>
    </div>
  </nav>
</template>
```

This template uses some boilerplate Bootstrap navigation bar code, as well as the atNavButton helper, which is part of the meteor-useraccounts package. This helper displays a "Sign In" button when the user is not logged in and it displays a "Sign Out" button when the user is logged in.

Finally, we need a layout for the list of clans. We'll see how this template is used in the next section, but for now, we'll make sure that /client/clans_layout.html contains the template shown in Listing 6-12:

Listing 6-12. Our template code for the clans layout

```
<template name="clansLayout">
  {{> yield region='nav'}}
  <div id="content">
    <div class="container">
      <div class="row">
        <div class="col-md-3">
          {{> yield region='clans'}}
        </div>
        <div class="col-md-9">
          {{> yield}}
        </div>
      </div>
    </div>
  </div>
</template>
```

Configurations

With the templates done, it's time to look at all of the configurations. First, we need to configure Account Templates by creating a new file: /lib/config/at_config.js, with the code shown in Listing 6-13:

Listing 6-13. The Account Templates configuration

```
AccountsTemplates.configure({
    showForgotPasswordLink: true,
    overrideLoginErrors: true,
    enablePasswordChange: true,
    negativeValidation: true,
    positiveValidation: true,
    negativeFeedback: false,
    positiveFeedback: true
})
```

Most of these settings are self-explanatory, but Account Templates has dozens upon dozens of configuration options: sendVerificationEmail, enforceEmailVerification, forbidClientAccountCreation, just to name a few. To familiarize yourself with the broad range of settings available, feel free to navigate to `https://github.com/meteor-useraccounts/core/blob/master/Guide.md#configuration-api`.

Secondly, we need to configure the routing and make sure that the wiring of the templates makes sense. We do this by modifying `/lib/router/routes.js` to contain the code shown in Listing 6-14:

Listing 6-14. The revised /lib/router/routes.js file

```
Router.configure({
  layoutTemplate: 'masterLayout',
  loadingTemplate: 'loading',
  notFoundTemplate: 'pageNotFound',
  yieldTemplates: {
    nav: {to: 'nav'},
    clans: {to: 'clans'}
  }
});

Router.map(function() {
  this.route('home', {
    path: '/',
    layoutTemplate: 'clansLayout'
  });

  this.route('/clans/:_id', {
    template: 'clan',
    layoutTemplate: 'clansLayout',
    name: 'clan.show',
    data: function () {
      return Clans.findOne({_id: this.params._id});
    }
  });
});

AccountsTemplates.configureRoute('changePwd');
AccountsTemplates.configureRoute('enrollAccount');
AccountsTemplates.configureRoute('forgotPwd');
AccountsTemplates.configureRoute('resetPwd');
AccountsTemplates.configureRoute('signIn');
AccountsTemplates.configureRoute('signUp');
AccountsTemplates.configureRoute('verifyEmail');
```

This configuration file has three main parts: the Iron Router default configuration, the Iron Router route mapping, and the Account Templates route mapping. We went over routing in Chapter 4, so the only alien part of this configuration file should be the list of `AccountTemplates.configureRoute(...)` calls. These calls are necessary if we want to use predefined `AccountTemplate` layouts for specific tasks.

For example, if we want to use the predefined "Sign Up" HTML template, we need to configure the "signUp" route, as we do above. There are a number of potential routes that can be configured. A list of them can be also found at the `https://github.com/meteor-useraccounts/core/blob/master/Guide.md#configuration-api`Github repository that I previously mentioned.

That's now all of the updates covered that we need to make to our clans.io project. The app should now be ready to run!

Deploying Your App

Now that we have a working app, it would be nice to deploy it somewhere in the cloud so we can share it with friends, family, or potential clients. We will go over two ways of deploying your Meteor app. As of this writing, both are free.

Deploying on Meteor.com

Deploying your app on meteor.com is incredibly easy. First, navigate to the root directory of your project, and then simply run the command:

```
meteor deploy your_app_name.meteor.com
```

Keep in mind that your app name needs to be unique. Once you finish the process, you can simply navigate to `http://your_app_name.meteor.com` and your app should be up and running in the cloud!

Deploying on Modulus.io

Modulus.io is a freemium service that offers Meteor hosting for free for up to a month. The deployment process is almost as easy as deploying on meteor.com and Modulus.io provides several tutorials on how to get started. After creating a Meteor app container on the Modulus.io dashboard and installing the Modulus.io command line interface utility, simply navigate to your project directory and run the command:

```
modulus deploy
```

After the upload process completes, your app URL will resemble `http://your_app-12345.onmodulus.net`. You can now share your project with the world!

Summary

Congratulations on completing and deploying your first Meteor app project. In this chapter, we've covered adding authentication to the clans.io app so that you can offer different services to users that are logged in and those that aren't. We also looked at ways to deploy your finished app to cloud.

I hope you've seen from this brief introductory guide just how easy Meteor makes the app-creation process, but also how powerful Meteor can be. The Meteor team has great plans for Meteor, and it's only going to become faster, more widely supported, and more feature-rich in future. I wish you the best of luck with creating your own Meteor projects.

Index

Get the eBook for only $5!

Why limit yourself?

Now you can take the weightless companion with you wherever you go and access your content on your PC, phone, tablet, or reader.

Since you've purchased this print book, we're happy to offer you the eBook in all 3 formats for just $5.

Convenient and fully searchable, the PDF version enables you to easily find and copy code—or perform examples by quickly toggling between instructions and applications. The MOBI format is ideal for your Kindle, while the ePUB can be utilized on a variety of mobile devices.

To learn more, go to www.apress.com/companion or contact support@apress.com.

Printed in the United States
By Bookmasters

THE OFFICIAL MIXER'S MANUAL